# The Ultimate Bangladeshi Cookbook

## 111 Dishes From Bangladesh To Cook Right Now

### Slavka Bodic

Imprint: Independently published

Please sign up for free Balkan and Mediterranean recipes:
www.balkanfood.org

# Introduction

Bangladeshi cuisine is a vibrant and diverse culinary tradition that reflects the country's rich history and cultural heritage. Located in South Asia, Bangladesh shares many similarities with its neighboring countries in terms of cuisine but also has its own distinct flavors and cooking styles. The cuisine is influenced by a range of factors, including the country's geography, climate, religion, and social customs. From spicy curries and flavorful rice dishes to delicious sweets and snacks, Bangladeshi cuisine is a treat for all as it offers a unique culinary experience to those who are willing to explore it.

Then this *Ultimate Bangladeshi Cookbook* is just the perfect read for you. Bangladeshi food, like its history and diverse culture, is far more interesting than you think. The cuisine offers lots of delicious desserts, salads, soups, appetizers, etc. All Bangladeshi recipes are prepared using a mix of rich and delicious ingredients using unique cooking techniques. What's most exciting about Bangladeshi cuisine is that it's considered highly nutritious, and by reading this cookbook, you'll know why!

Experiencing Bangladeshi cuisine and learning to cook various Bangladeshi meals was one thing that I wanted to share with all my avid cookbook readers. And this cookbook comes after my seven years of learning about the diverse Bangladeshi culinary culture. All the 111 recipes shared in this cookbook are enough to create an entire Bangladeshi menu of your own. With these recipes, you can enjoy special flavors on special occasions, or you can just surprise your loved ones with authentic Bangladeshi flavors.

What you can find in this cookbook:

- Something about the Bangladesh and Bangladeshi cuisine
- Bangladeshi Breakfast recipes
- Snacks
- Sides and salad recipes
- Soup recipes
- Main dishes and entrees
- Bangladeshi desserts and drinks

Let's try all these Bangladeshi Recipes and recreate a complete menu to celebrate the amazing Bangladeshi flavors and aromas!

# TABLE OF CONTENTS

# Why Bangladeshi Cuisine?

Bangladeshi cuisine is a mix of flavors, aromas, and textures that are unique to the region. The cuisine is influenced by the country's geography, climate, and historical events that have shaped its culture over the centuries. The cuisine of Bangladesh is a perfect blend of Mughlai, Middle Eastern, and South Asian flavors. The country's cuisine offers a wide range of dishes with varying levels of spiciness and ingredients that are used in different parts and regions of the country.

One of the most common staples in Bangladeshi cuisine is rice, which is consumed in various forms and is the basis of many dishes. The country's rice varieties range from aromatic to non-aromatic and are used for different dishes. Bangladesh is also known for its seafood, especially in the coastal regions, where fish and other seafood are a staple. In Bangladesh, a typical meal consists of rice, lentils, vegetables, and a protein source. The protein source can be anything from chicken, beef, mutton, fish, or eggs. The meal is usually accompanied by various condiments and pickles that add flavor and texture to the dish. Some of the most popular dishes in Bangladeshi cuisine include:

- **Biriyani:** Aromatic and flavorful rice dish made with a mix of spices, meat, or vegetables. Biriyani is a popular dish served during festivals and celebrations.
- **Fish Curry:** A staple in coastal regions, fish curry is made with various types of fish cooked in a spicy tomato-based gravy.

- **Shorshe Ilish:** A signature dish of Bangladesh made with Hilsa fish cooked in mustard gravy. This dish is a delicacy and is typically served during weddings and other special occasions.
- **Chingri Malai Curry:** A creamy and mild curry made with prawns, coconut milk, and spices.
- **Beef Rezala:** A rich and creamy beef curry made with yogurt, spices, and a touch of sweetness.
- **Dal:** A lentil-based soup made with different types of lentils and flavored with spices and herbs. Dal is a common dish in Bangladeshi cuisine and is usually served with rice.
- **Pitha:** A type of sweet or savory cake made with some rice flour and stuffed with coconut, jaggery, or meat. Pitha is a popular snack during winter and is a staple during festivals.
- **Chotpoti:** A spicy and tangy street food made with mashed potatoes, chickpeas, tamarind sauce, and various spices. This dish is usually served in small bowls and is a popular snack in Bangladesh.
- **Samosas:** A popular snack in Bangladesh, samosas are fried pastries filled with spiced vegetables, chicken, or beef.
- **Borhani:** A spicy and tangy drink made with yogurt, mint, and various spices. Borhani is usually served during special occasions and is a popular drink in Bangladesh.

Bangladesh has a rich culinary heritage that has evolved over the centuries. The cuisine is a perfect blend of different cultures and is a testament to the country's diverse history. With its use of aromatic spices, fresh seafood, and varied cooking techniques, Bangladeshi cuisine is a feast for the senses and is gaining popularity worldwide.

# Bangladesh

Over the centuries, Bangladesh has been influenced by various cultures and historical events, resulting in a diverse and rich heritage. The country's population of more than 164 million people makes it the eighth most populous nation globally. The majority of the population identify as Bengali Muslims, but there are also significant minority groups of Hindus, Buddhists, and Christians. The official language of Bangladesh is Bengali, spoken by the vast majority of its citizens, while English is also widely spoken.

Following a nine-month war, Bangladesh achieved independence from Pakistan in 1971. Since then, the country has made noteworthy progress in various fields such as medical, healthcare, education, and reducing poverty. However, Bangladesh still grapples with a set of challenges including political instability, corruption, and natural disasters such as cyclones and floods. The country's economy has witnessed substantial changes in recent years, with a shift from an agricultural-based economy to a more diversified one. The garment industry has emerged as a major contributor to the economy, and Bangladesh now stands as the world's second-largest exporter of garments. Furthermore, the country's agricultural sector is a significant producer of products such as rice, jute, and tea.

It really has a rich cultural heritage, with a variety of traditions that reflect the country's history and diversity. The arts, music, and literature have always been an important part of Bangladeshi culture, and the country has produced many notable writers, musicians, and artists. One of the most distinctive features of Bangladeshi culture is its food. Bangladeshi cuisine is characterized by its rich, spicy flavors and its use of a great variety of herbs and spices. Rice is the staple in the country, and is often served with curries and lentil dishes. Seafood is also popular, with fish and prawns featuring prominently in many dishes.

One of the most popular dishes in this country is biryani, a spicy rice dish that is usually made with meat, fish, or vegetables. Another popular dish is dal, a lentil-based curry that's often enjoyed with rice or bread. Fish curries are also common, with hilsa being a particularly popular fish in Bangladesh. Bangladeshi cuisine also features a variety of sweet dishes, including Rasgulla, a sweet cheese ball that's soaked in syrup, and Sondesh, a sweet made from milk and sugar. Tea is another beverage and is regularly served with milk and sugar.

# Breakfast

# Paratha

**Preparation time:** 15 minutes
**Cook time:** 35 minutes
**Nutrition facts (per serving):** 152 Cal (4.9g fat, 5.2g protein, 3g fiber)

Paratha is a popular unleavened flatbread from the Indian subcontinent, made by pan-frying whole wheat dough with ghee or oil.

**Ingredients (4 servings)**
2 cups of wheat flour
½ teaspoon of salt
1 tablespoon of oil or ghee (clarified butter)
Water, as needed
Extra flour, for dusting
Oil or ghee, for cooking

**Preparation**
In a suitable mixing bowl, combine the wheat flour, salt, and 1 tablespoon of oil or ghee. Mix. Slowly pour in water and knead the prepared dough until it becomes smooth and pliable. Once the prepared dough is well-kneaded, cover it with some damp cloth or plastic wrap and leave it to rest for about 20 minutes. After resting, divide the prepared dough into small lemon-sized balls. Spread each ball between your palms to make a smooth round ball. Take 1 dough ball and flatten it slightly with your fingers.

Dip it into flour to prevent sticking and spread it out into a thin circle with your rolling pin. Apply a little bit oil or ghee on the surface of the rolled dough circle. Now, make pleats by folding the prepared dough in a series of pleats, like a fan or an accordion, until you reach the end. Coil the pleated dough into a spiral shape, tucking the end underneath. Press it down gently with your fingers to form a suitable round disc. Dust the disc with flour and roll it out again gently into a slightly thicker circle, about 6-7 inches in diameter. Heat a suitable griddle or a non-stick pan over medium heat. Place your rolled paratha on the hot griddle and cook for about 1-2 minutes until small bubbles start to form on the surface. Flip the paratha and apply some oil or ghee on the cooked side.

Continue cooking for 1-2 minutes until golden spots appear on both sides, pressing gently with a spatula to help the paratha puff up. Remove the cooked paratha from the griddle and place it on a plate. Repeat this whole process with its remaining dough balls to make more parathas. Serve hot with your favorite side dish, such as curry, chutney, or yogurt. Enjoy your delicious homemade parathas!

# Luchi

**Preparation time:** 15 minutes
**Cook time:** 35 minutes
**Nutrition facts (per serving):** 325 Cal (17g fat, 13g protein, 1.2g fiber)

Luchi is a popular deep-fried puffed bread that is commonly served as a breakfast meal in Bangladesh. It's made from flour and is similar to puri in Indian cuisine.

**Ingredients (4 servings)**
2 cups of all-purpose flour
1 teaspoon of salt
2 tablespoons of ghee or oil
Water, as needed
Oil or ghee, for deep frying

**Preparation**
In a suitable mixing bowl, sift the all-purpose flour to remove any lumps. Add the salt and ghee or oil to the flour. Mix. Slowly pour in water, little by little, and knead the prepared dough until it becomes smooth and elastic. The prepared dough should not be too soft or too firm, but pliable enough to roll out. Cover the prepared dough with some damp cloth and leave for about 20 minutes. Heat enough oil or ghee in a suitable deep frying pan over medium heat for frying. Divide the prepared dough into small lemon-sized balls.

Take 1 dough ball and roll it into a suitable circle using a rolling pin. The size should be about 3-4 inches in diameter. Carefully slide the rolled dough circle into the hot oil or ghee for frying. Press gently with a slotted spoon to help it puff up. Fry the Luchi until it turns golden in color and puffs up fully, flipping it once or twice. Remove the fried Luchi from the oil or ghee using any slotted spoon and place it on a (paper towel-lined) plate properly to absorb any excess oil or ghee. Repeat this whole process with its remaining dough balls, rolling them out and frying them one by one. Serve hot and crispy Luchi with your favorite side dishes, such as Cholar Dal (Bengali-style lentil curry), Aloo Dum (spiced potato curry), or any other curry of your choice.

# Pitha

**Preparation time:** 15 minutes
**Cook time:** 35 minutes
**Nutrition facts (per serving):** 167 Cal (5.3 fat, 11.4 protein, 0.8g fiber)

Pitha is a popular traditional Bengali rice cake that's typically made during festivals or special occasions. There are various types of Pitha, and here's a simple recipe for making one type called "Chaler Pitha," which is a steamed rice cake flavored with jaggery and coconut.

## Ingredients (4 servings)
### Rice Cake
1 cup of rice flour
½ cup of jaggery, grated or finely chopped
½ cup of coconut, grated
½ teaspoon of cardamom powder
A pinch of salt
Water, as needed

### Steaming
Water, as needed
Banana leaves or parchment paper, for lining

## Preparation
Wash the rice flour thoroughly with water to remove any impurities. Drain and keep aside. In a suitable mixing bowl, combine the grated jaggery, grated coconut, cardamom powder, and a pinch of salt. Mix. Add the washed rice flour to the bowl and mix everything to make a dough. If

the prepared dough feels too dry, you can add a little water, slowly, to make a soft, pliable dough. Once the prepared dough is well-mixed, cover it with some damp cloth or plastic wrap and leave for almost 20 minutes. This helps to allow the flavors to meld and the prepared dough to settle. While the prepared dough is resting, prepare the steamer.

Fill a steamer pot or a suitable pot with water and cook it to a boil. Line the steamer basket with banana leaves or parchment paper to prevent sticking. After resting, take a suitable portion of the prepared dough and shape it into a suitable round or oval disc, about ½ inch in thickness. You can shape it using your hands or by using a cookie cutter. Place the shaped rice cake on the lined steamer basket then cover it with a lid. Steam the rice cake for about 10-15 minutes on medium heat until cooked through and firm to touch. Once cooked, carefully remove the rice cake from the steamer and let it cool slightly. Repeat this whole process with its remaining dough to make more rice cakes. Serve the warm Chaler Pitha as a breakfast or snack, and enjoy the delicious combination of jaggery, coconut, and rice flavors!

# Chapor Ghonto

**Preparation time:** 15 minutes
**Cook time:** 35 minutes
**Nutrition facts (per serving):** 334 Cal (31g fat, 6g protein, 0.1g fiber)

Chapor Ghonto is a popular mixed vegetable curry from Bengali cuisine that's made with a medley of vegetables and lentil fritters.

**Ingredients (4 servings)**
*Lentil Fritters (Bori)*
½ cup of split black gram lentil (urad dal)
½ teaspoon of cumin seeds
½ teaspoon of turmeric powder
½ teaspoon of red chili powder
Salt, to taste
Oil, for deep frying

*Curry*
1 cup of mixed vegetables (potatoes, carrots, cauliflower, beans, peas)
½ cup of onions, chopped
½ cup of tomatoes, chopped
½ teaspoon of cumin seeds
½ teaspoon of ginger paste
½ teaspoon of garlic paste
½ teaspoon of turmeric powder
½ teaspoon of red chili powder
½ teaspoon of cumin powder
½ teaspoon of coriander powder

½ teaspoon of garam masala

Salt, to taste

2 tablespoons of oil

Fresh coriander leaves, for garnish

## Preparation

### *Lentil Fritters (Bori)*

Soak the split black gram lentil (urad dal) in water for about 4-5 hours. Drain the soaked lentils and grind them to a smooth paste in a suitable blender or food processor. Add cumin seeds, turmeric powder, red chili powder, and salt to the lentil paste. Mix. Heat oil in a suitable deep frying pan over medium heat. Drop small portions of the lentil paste into the hot oil. Fry the lentil fritters until golden and crispy.

### *Curry*

Heat the oil in a suitable pan or Kadhai over medium heat. Stir in cumin seeds and let them cook for 30 seconds. Toss in chopped onions and sauté until golden. Add ginger paste and garlic paste. Sauté for a minute. Toss in chopped tomatoes and cook until they turn soft and mushy. Stir in turmeric powder, red chili powder, cumin powder, coriander powder, and salt. Mix. Add the mixed vegetables and sauté for a few minutes. Add a little bit of water, cover the pan, and let the vegetables cook until tender. Add the fried lentil fritters (Bori) and garam masala. Mix gently. Continue cooking for couple of minutes, with occasional stirring. Garnish with coriander leaves. Serve hot Chapor Ghonto with rice or flatbreads as a delicious and nutritious mixed vegetable curry dish from Bengali cuisine.

# Beguni

**Preparation time:** 15 minutes
**Cook time:** 35 minutes
**Nutrition facts (per serving):** 162 Cal (2.8g fat, 7.5g protein, 1g fiber)

Beguni is a popular Bengali street food made with deep-fried eggplant slices coated with spiced gram flour (chickpea flour) batter. It's a crispy and delicious snack to serve at every table.

## Ingredients (4 servings)
1 medium-sized eggplant (brinjal/aubergine), washed and thinly sliced
1 cup of gram flour (chickpea flour/besan)
½ teaspoon of turmeric powder
½ teaspoon of red chili powder
½ teaspoon of cumin powder
½ teaspoon of coriander powder
¼ teaspoon of baking soda
Salt, to taste
Water, as needed
Oil, for deep frying

## Preparation
### Eggplant Slices
Wash the eggplant and pat dry with a clean cloth. Slice the eggplant into thin rounds or strips about ¼ inch thick. Place the eggplant slices in a suitable bowl filled water and a little bit of salt then leave them to soak for almost 10 minutes. Drain the water and pat dry the eggplant slices using any clean cloth or paper towel.

### Batter

In a suitable mixing bowl, add gram flour (chickpea flour), turmeric powder, red chili powder, cumin powder, coriander powder, baking soda, and salt. Mix. Slowly pour in water and whisk until you get a smooth and thick batter. Coat and Fry the Eggplant Slices: Heat oil in a suitable deep frying pan over medium heat. Dip each eggplant slice into the prepared batter, coating it evenly on both sides. Gently slide the coated eggplant slice into the hot oil and deep-fry until golden and crispy on both sides. Remove the fried Beguni using any slotted spoon and spread them on paper towels to absorb excess oil.

Serve the hot and crispy Beguni as a snack or side dish with mint chutney or ketchup. Beguni is best served immediately after frying to enjoy its crispy texture.

# Haleem

**Preparation time:** 15 minutes
**Cook time:** 35 minutes
**Nutrition facts (per serving):** 420 Cal (3.6gfat, 24.2g protein, 0.6g fiber)

Haleem is a rich and flavorful thick stew made with lentils, meat (usually beef or mutton), and a blend of spices. It's a popular dish in many Middle Eastern, South Asian, and Central Asian countries, including Bangladesh. Haleem is typically slow-cooked for hours to develop its complex flavors and create a thick, creamy consistency.

## Ingredients (4 servings)
1 cup of mixed lentils (whole wheat, barley, yellow split lentils, and red lentils), washed and soaked
½ lb. of meat (beef or mutton), boneless or with bones, cut into small pieces
½ cup of broken wheat
1 large onion, finely chopped
3 cloves of garlic, minced
1-inch piece of ginger, minced
3 green chilies, finely chopped (optional)
½ teaspoon of turmeric powder
1 teaspoon of red chili powder
1 teaspoon of cumin powder
1 teaspoon of coriander powder
½ teaspoon of garam masala powder
¼ teaspoon of cinnamon powder

¼ teaspoon of cardamom powder

¼ teaspoon of nutmeg powder

Salt, to taste

2 tablespoons of ghee or oil

### Garnish

Fried onions, to taste

Chopped fresh cilantro (coriander) leaves, to taste

Lemon wedges, to taste

Ginger julienne, to taste

Garam masala powder, to taste

## Preparation

### Lentils and Meat

In a suitable pot, add the soaked lentils, broken wheat, and meat, along with enough water to cover them. Cook to a boil. Reduce its heat to low and simmer, covered, for about 2-3 hours until the lentils and meat are fully cooked and tender. Once cooked, use a hand blender or a potato masher to partially mash the lentils and meat to create a thick, creamy texture. Set aside.

### Spice Mix

In a suitable bowl, mix together the turmeric powder, red chili powder, cumin powder, coriander powder, garam masala powder, cinnamon powder, cardamom powder, nutmeg powder, and salt to form a spice mix. Set aside.

### Tadka (Tempering)

Heat the ghee or the oil in a separate pan over medium heat. Toss in the chopped onions and sauté until golden. Add the minced garlic, minced ginger, and green chilies (if using) and sauté for another 2-3 minutes until fragrant.

### *Combine and Simmer*

Add the spice mix prepared in Step 2 to the tadka (tempering) and stir well. Add the mashed lentils and meat mixture to the pan with the tadka (tempering) and mix everything together. Simmer the Haleem on low heat for another 30-40 minutes, with occasional stirring to prevent sticking to the bottom of the pan.

Ladle the hot Haleem into serving bowls. Garnish with fried onions, chopped cilantro, ginger julienne, a sprinkle of garam masala powder, and a squeeze of lemon juice. Serve hot with naan, roti, or rice.

# Bhuna Khichuri

**Preparation time:** 15 minutes
**Cook time:** 35 minutes
**Nutrition facts (per serving):** 335 Cal (3.8g fat, 6.8g protein, 1.4g fiber)

Bhuna Khichuri is a hearty and flavorful dish made with rice and lentils, often enjoyed as comfort food in Bangladesh. It's typically prepared by slow-cooking rice and lentils with a mix of spices and vegetables to create a rich and aromatic one-pot meal.

**Ingredients (4 servings)**
1 cup of Basmati rice, soaked then rinsed
½ cup of split yellow lentils (Moong Dal), washed and soaked
½ cup of mixed vegetables (carrots, peas, and potatoes), chopped
1 large onion, finely chopped
2-3 cloves of garlic, minced
1 inch piece of ginger, minced
2-3 green chilies, slit (optional)
½ teaspoon of turmeric powder
½ teaspoon of cumin seeds
½ teaspoon of coriander powder
½ teaspoon of cumin powder
½ teaspoon of red chili powder
½ teaspoon of garam masala powder
Salt, to taste
2 tablespoons of oil
Fresh cilantro (coriander) leaves, chopped, for garnish
Lemon wedges, for serving

## Preparation

Heat the oil or the ghee in a suitable pot or pressure cooker over medium heat. Stir the cumin seeds and let them splutter. Toss in the chopped onions and sauté until golden. Add the minced garlic, minced ginger, and green chilies (if using) and sauté for another 2-3 minutes until fragrant. Add the mixed vegetables and sauté for 3-4 minutes until slightly softened. Add the turmeric powder, coriander and cumin powder, and red chili powder. Mix.

Drain your soaked rice and lentils and add them to the pot. Stir well to coat the rice and lentils with the spices. Stir in enough water to cover the rice and lentils, usually around 4 cups. Adjust the water quantity based on your desired consistency. Cook the prepared mixture to a boil. If using a pressure cooker, close the lid and pressure cook it for 2-3 whistles. If using a regular pot, cover with a lid and cook on a simmer on low heat until the rice and lentils are fully cooked, and the vegetables are soft, occasionally stir.

Once the Bhuna Khichuri is cooked, sprinkle garam masala powder and mix gently. Garnish with chopped cilantro leaves. Serve hot with lemon wedges, and enjoy this delicious and comforting Bhuna Khichuri on its own or with some side of your choice, such as papad, pickle, or yogurt.

# Bhorta

**Preparation time:** 15 minutes
**Cook time:** 35 minutes
**Nutrition facts (per serving):** 218 Cal (2g fat, 24.5g protein, 3.2g fiber)

Bhorta is a popular Bengali dish that consists of mashed vegetables, typically served as a side dish or condiment with rice, bread, or flatbreads. It's often seasoned with spices, herbs, and mustard oil, which gives it a unique and delicious taste.

## Ingredients (4 servings)

2 cups of mixed vegetables (boiled potatoes, roasted eggplant, boiled peas, boiled carrots)
1 small onion, finely chopped
2-3 green chilies, finely chopped
½ teaspoon of turmeric powder
½ teaspoon of red chili powder (optional)
½ teaspoon of cumin powder
½ teaspoon of mustard or regular oil
Salt, to taste
Chopped cilantro (coriander leaves), for garnish

## Preparation

If using raw vegetables, peel and chop them into small pieces. Boil or roast them until soft and cooked. If using leftover boiled vegetables, skip this step. In a suitable mixing bowl, add the cooked vegetables and mash them using a fork, potato masher, until well mashed. Add the finely chopped onion, green chilies, turmeric powder, red chili powder, cumin powder, mustard oil (or regular cooking oil), and salt to taste. Mix. Garnish with chopped cilantro (coriander leaves). Serve Bhorta as a side dish or condiment with rice, bread, or flatbreads such as roti, paratha, or naan.

# Jilapi

**Preparation time**: 15 minutes
**Cook time:** 35 minutes
**Nutrition facts (per serving):** 248 Cal (1g fat, 4.5g protein, 3.1g fiber)

Jilapi, also known as Jalebi, is a popular sweet, deep-fried dessert that's commonly enjoyed in Bangladesh and many other South Asian countries. It's made by deep-frying a fermented flour batter into pretzel or spiral shapes, which are then soaked in a prepared sugar syrup flavored with cardamom or saffron. Jilapi is known for its crispy texture and sweet, syrupy taste.

## Ingredients (4 servings)
### Batter
1 cup of all-purpose flour
1 tablespoon of cornstarch
½ teaspoon of baking powder
½ cup of plain yogurt
¼ teaspoon of turmeric powder (for color, optional)
Water, as needed for making a thick, smooth batter

### Sugar Syrup
1 cup of sugar
½ cup of water
¼ teaspoon of cardamom powder or a few strands of saffron (for flavor)
1 teaspoon of lemon juice

Oil, for deep frying

## Preparation

In a suitable mixing bowl, sift the all-purpose flour to remove any lumps. Add cornstarch, baking powder, plain yogurt, and turmeric powder (if using) to the flour. Mix. Slowly pour in water, little by little, and whisk this batter until it becomes thick and smooth. This batter should have a pouring consistency, similar to pancake batter. Cover this batter with a clean cloth and let it ferment for at least 4-5 hours, or overnight for best results. The fermentation process will help create air bubbles in the batter, giving the Jilapi its characteristic texture.

### *Sugar syrup*

Add sugar to water in a saucepan over medium heat. Add cardamom powder or saffron strands for flavor. Cook the sugar syrup to a boil, then reduce its heat and Cook it on a simmer for about 5-7 minutes until it reaches a slightly sticky consistency. Stir in the lemon juice to prevent crystallization. Remove from heat and set aside. Once this batter is fermented, heat oil in a suitable deep frying pan over medium heat for frying.

Using a Jilapi funnel or a plastic squeeze bottle with a suitable nozzle, carefully drizzle this batter in pretzel or spiral shapes into the hot oil. Fry the Jilapi until golden in color and crispy, flipping them once or twice. Remove the fried Jilapi from the oil using any slotted spoon and drain the excess oil. Immediately dip the hot Jilapi into the prepared sugar syrup, letting them soak for a few seconds to absorb the syrup. Remove the soaked Jilapi from the sugar syrup and spread them on a serving plate to cool down. Repeat this whole process with the remaining batter, frying and soaking the Jilapi in batches. Serve Jilapi warm or at room temperature as a sweet and indulgent dessert.

# Puri

**Preparation time:** 15 minutes
**Cook time:** 35 minutes
**Nutrition facts (per serving):** 139 Cal (11.5g fat, 7.1g protein, 0g fiber)

Puri is a popular deep-fried bread that's commonly enjoyed in Bangladesh and many other South Asian countries. It's made from a simple wheat flour dough that is rolled out into small rounds and deep-fried until it puffs up into a light, crispy bread. Puri is often served with various curries, chutneys, or as part of a festive meal.

## Ingredients (4 servings)
2 cups of all-purpose flour
½ teaspoon of salt
1 tablespoon of oil
¾ cup of water
Oil, for deep frying

## Preparation
In a suitable mixing bowl, sift the all-purpose flour to remove any lumps. Stir in salt and oil to the flour and Mix. Slowly pour in water, and knead the prepared dough until smooth and elastic dough. The prepared dough should not be too soft or too stiff. Cover the prepared dough with a clean cloth and leave for about 20 minutes. Heat oil in a suitable deep frying pan over medium heat for frying. Divide the prepared dough into small lemon-sized balls. Roll out each ball into a suitable round disc, about 3-4 inches in diameter, using a rolling pin. You can dust the work surface and the prepared dough with a little flour to prevent sticking.

Add the rolled-out dough into the hot oil and press it gently with a slotted spoon or a ladle to help it puff up. Fry the Puri until it puffs up and turns golden in color on both sides, flipping it once or twice. Remove the fried Puri from the oil using any slotted spoon and drain the excess oil. Place the fried Puri on a (paper towel-lined) plate to absorb any excess oil. Repeat this entire process with the remaining dough, frying the Puris in batches. Serve the hot and crispy Puri immediately with your favorite curry, chutney, or side dish.

# Chhola'r Dal

**Preparation time:** 15 minutes
**Cook time:** 35 minutes
**Nutrition facts (per serving):** 209 Cal (4.7g fat, 7.8g protein, 2g fiber)

Chhola'r Dal, also known as Chana Dal, is a popular Bengali dish made with split Bengal gram lentils. It's a flavorful and comforting lentil dish that's often served with rice or flatbreads.

## Ingredients (4 servings)

1 cup of chana dal (Bengal gram lentils)
2 tablespoons of oil or ghee
1 teaspoon of cumin seeds
1 bay leaf
1 cinnamon stick
3 green cardamom pods, slightly crushed
3 cloves
1 medium-sized onion, finely chopped
1 teaspoon of ginger paste
1 teaspoon of garlic paste
½ teaspoon of turmeric powder
½ teaspoon of red chili powder (adjust to taste)
1 teaspoon of cumin powder
1 teaspoon of coriander powder
Salt, to taste
3 cups of water (or as needed)
Chopped coriander leaves, for garnish

## Preparation

Wash the chana dal thoroughly under running water until the water runs clear. Warm up the oil or ghee in a pressure cooker or a heavy-bottomed pot over medium heat. Add the cumin seeds, bay leaf, cinnamon stick, cardamom pods, and cloves to the hot oil or ghee. Sauté for a minute or until fragrant. Toss in the chopped onion and sauté until it turns golden in color. Add the ginger paste and garlic paste to the pot and sauté for another minute.

Drain the soaked chana dal and transfer it to the pot. Stir well. Stir in turmeric powder, red chili powder, cumin powder, coriander powder, and salt to this pot. Mix to coat the lentils with the spices. Pour water in to your pot and cook it to a boil. If using your pressure cooker, close the lid and cook the dal for about 4-5 whistles. If using a pot, cover it with a lid and cook on a simmer on low heat until the lentils are soft and fully cooked, with occasional stirring and adding more water if needed. Once the lentils are cooked, check for seasoning and adjust, as needed. Garnish the Chhola'r Dal with chopped coriander leaves and remove from heat. Serve hot with rice, roti, or any flatbread of your choice.

# Shorshe Ilish

**Preparation time:** 15 minutes

**Cook time:** 35 minutes

**Nutrition facts (per serving):** 255 Cal (5g fat, 18.5g protein, 1.5g fiber)

Shorshe Ilish, also known as Hilsa fish cooked in mustard sauce, is a popular Bengali dish that's loved for its distinct flavors and unique taste.

## Ingredients (4 servings)

4 pieces of Hilsa fish (Ilish) steaks

2 tablespoons of mustard seeds

1 tablespoon of poppy seeds

2 green chilies, chopped

½ teaspoon of turmeric powder

½ teaspoon of red chili powder (optional)

½ teaspoon of salt

½ teaspoon of sugar (optional)

1 tablespoon of mustard oil

1 tablespoon of oil (preferably mustard oil)

Fresh coriander leaves, for garnish

## Preparation

Rub the fish steaks with a little turmeric powder and keep aside. In a grinder or blender, add mustard seeds, poppy seeds, and green chilies. Grind into a smooth paste by adding a little water if needed. Heat mustard oil in a suitable pan or kadai over medium heat. Add the fish steaks and fry them on both sides until lightly golden. Remove the fish steaks from the pan and keep aside. In that same pan, warm up 1 tablespoon of oil (preferably mustard oil), if needed. Add the mustard-poppy seed paste to the pan and sauté for a minute. Stir in turmeric powder, red chili powder (if using), salt, and sugar (if using) to the pan. Mix. Add about ½ cup of water to this pan and cook it to a boil. Add the fried fish steaks back to the pan. Cook the fish in the mustard sauce for about 5-6 minutes. Once your fish is cooked, turn off its heat and drizzle some mustard oil over the top for extra flavor (optional).Garnish the Shorshe Ilish with freshly chopped coriander leaves. Serve hot.

# Snacks

# Singara

**Preparation time:** 15 minutes
**Cook time:** 35 minutes
**Nutrition facts (per serving):** 258 Cal (9g fat, 1g protein, 4g fiber)

Singara, a popular Bangladeshi snack that's similar to a samosa. Singara is a deep-fried pastry filled with spiced vegetables, and it's perfect for enjoying with a cup of tea or as a tasty appetizer.

## Ingredients (3 servings)
### Dough
1 cup all-purpose flour
¼ teaspoon salt
2 tablespoons oil
¼ cup water

### Filling
1 medium potato, boiled and peeled
½ cup peas, boiled
½ cup carrots, finely chopped and boiled
½ cup onions, finely chopped
2-3 green chilies, finely chopped
½ teaspoon ginger paste
½ teaspoon garlic paste
½ teaspoon cumin seeds
½ teaspoon coriander powder
½ teaspoon turmeric powder
½ teaspoon red chili powder

½ teaspoon garam masala powder

Salt, to taste

2 tablespoons oil for cooking

Oil, for deep frying

**Preparation**

In a suitable mixing bowl, combine the all-purpose flour, salt, and oil.. Gradually pour in water and knead the mixture into a smooth and pliable dough. Cover the prepared dough with some damp cloth and leave it to sit for 20 minutes. Meanwhile, prepare the filling. Heat 2 tablespoons of oil in a suitable pan over medium heat. Add cumin seeds and let them splutter. Then toss in the finely chopped onions and sauté until they turn golden in color. Stir in ginger paste and garlic paste, and sauté for a minute.

Add the boiled and peeled potato, boiled peas, and boiled carrots to the pan. Mash the potato slightly with a spatula. Add turmeric powder, coriander powder, red chili powder, garam masala powder, and salt to taste. Mix and sauté for 2-3 minutes. Turn off its heat and allow the filling cool to room temperature. After the prepared dough has rested, divide it into small lemon-sized balls. Spread out each ball into a thin circular disc. Place a spoonful of the cooled vegetable filling in the center of the disc. Fold the disc into a triangular shape, sealing the edges tightly with a little water to form a samosa-like shape. Repeat this whole process with its remaining dough balls and filling. Heat oil in a suitable deep frying pan or kadai over medium heat. Carefully slide in the prepared Singara into the hot oil and fry them until golden in color and crispy from all sides. Serve.

# Pakora

**Preparation time:** 15 minutes
**Cook time:** 35 minutes
**Nutrition facts (per serving):** 275 Cal (7g fat, 6g protein, 2g fiber)

Pakora, a popular deep-fried vegetable fritter that's commonly enjoyed as a snack in Bangladesh and other South Asian countries. Pakoras are made by coating vegetables in a spiced chickpea flour batter and then deep frying them to crispy perfection.

## Ingredients (4 servings)

1 cup chickpea flour (besan)
½ cup water
1 small onion, thinly sliced
1 small potato, peeled and thinly sliced
½ cup spinach leaves, chopped
½ cup cauliflower florets
½ teaspoon cumin seeds
½ teaspoon carom seeds (Ajwain)
½ teaspoon red chili powder
½ teaspoon turmeric powder
½ teaspoon coriander powder
½ teaspoon garam masala powder
Salt, to taste
Oil, for deep frying

**Preparation**

In a suitable mixing bowl, combine the chickpea flour, water, cumin seeds, carom seeds, red chili powder, turmeric powder, coriander powder, garam masala powder, and salt to taste. Mix to make a nice smooth batter of pouring consistency. Add the thinly sliced onion, potato, chopped spinach, and cauliflower florets to the batter. Mix to coat the vegetables evenly with the batter. Heat the oil in a suitable deep frying pan or kadai over medium heat. Carefully drop spoonfuls of the vegetable-batter mixture into the hot oil and fry until golden in color and crispy from all sides. Using a slotted spoon, remove the cooked pakoras from the oil. Serve hot!

# Fuchka

**Preparation time:** 15 minutes
**Cook time:** 35 minutes
**Nutrition facts (per serving):** 207 Cal (14g fat, 7g protein, 1g fiber)

Fuchka, also known as Pani Puri or Golgappa in different regions of South Asia, is a popular street food and snack in Bangladesh. It consists of crispy hollow puris filled with spicy tangy tamarind water, chickpeas, and a variety of spices.

## Ingredients (4 servings)
### Puris
1 cup semolina (sooji or Rava)
¼ cup all-purpose flour (maida)
¼ teaspoon baking soda
Salt, to taste
Water, as needed
Oil, for deep frying

### Filling
1 cup boiled chickpeas (chana)
1 small onion, finely chopped
1 small potato, boiled and chopped
½ cup fresh coriander leaves, chopped
½ cup tamarind chutney (imli chutney)
½ teaspoon roasted cumin powder
½ teaspoon red chili powder
½ teaspoon chaat masala
Salt, to taste

**Preparation**

*Puris*

In a suitable mixing bowl, combine semolina, all-purpose flour, baking soda, and salt. Slowly pour in water and knead into a smooth and firm dough. Cover the prepared dough with some damp cloth and leave for almost 20 minutes. After resting, knead the prepared dough again for a few minutes to make it smooth. Divide the prepared dough into small lemon-sized balls. Spread out each ball into a thin disc using a rolling pin. You can use a little dry flour to dust while rolling to prevent sticking. Heat the oil in a suitable deep frying pan or kadai over medium heat. Carefully slide one rolled puri into the hot oil and press gently with a slotted spoon so that it puffs up. Flip and fry until golden and crispy. Repeat this whole process with the remaining puris. Once the puris are fried, transfer them onto a (paper towel-lined) plate.

*Filling*

In a suitable mixing bowl, combine boiled chickpeas, chopped onion, boiled potato, chopped coriander leaves, roasted cumin powder, red chili powder, chaat masala, and salt to taste. Mix. To assemble, gently tap a hole in the center of each puri using your thumb or the back of a spoon. Fill the puris with a spoonful of the chickpea filling. Drizzle some tamarind chutney on top of the filling in each Puri. Serve immediately and enjoy the crispy and tangy fuchka as a popular Bangladeshi street food snack!

# Jhalmuri

**Preparation time:** 15 minutes

**Cook time:** 35 minutes

**Nutrition facts (per serving):** 132 Cal (4g fat, 4g protein, 1.3g fiber)

Jhalmuri is a popular street food in Bangladesh, made with puffed rice, vegetables, and tangy spices. It's a flavorful and crunchy snack that's loved by many.

## Ingredients (4 Servings)

2 cups puffed rice

1 small onion, finely chopped

1 small tomato, finely chopped

1 small cucumber, finely chopped

1 small carrot, grated

1 small boiled potato, diced

½ cup roasted peanuts

½ cup sev (crunchy chickpea flour noodles)

2 tablespoons fresh coriander leaves, chopped

1 tablespoon fresh mint leaves, chopped (optional)

1 tablespoon mustard oil or vegetable oil

1 tablespoon tamarind chutney

1 teaspoon chaat masala

½ teaspoon roasted cumin powder

½ teaspoon red chili powder

Salt, to taste

## Preparation

In a suitable mixing bowl, combine the puffed rice, chopped onion, chopped tomato, chopped cucumber, grated carrot, diced boiled potato, roasted peanuts, sev, chopped coriander leaves, and mint leaves (if using). Add the mustard oil or vegetable oil to the bowl and toss all the ingredients gently to coat them with the oil. Add the tamarind chutney, chaat masala, roasted cumin powder, red chili powder, and salt to taste. Mix. Serve immediately and enjoy the tangy and spicy flavors of Jhalmuri as a popular Bangladeshi street food snack!

# Chotpoti

**Preparation time:** 15 minutes
**Cook time:** 35 minutes
**Nutrition facts (per serving):** 221 Cal (12g fat, 3.2g protein, 4g fiber)

Chotpoti is a popular Bangladeshi street food that's a tangy and spicy combination of mashed chickpeas, tamarind water, and spices. It's typically served with crispy puris and makes for a flavorful and satisfying snack.

**Ingredients (4 servings)**
*Chotpoti*
1 cup boiled chickpeas (chana), mashed
1 small onion, finely chopped
1 small tomato, finely chopped
1 small cucumber, finely chopped
1 small green chili, finely chopped
½ cup tamarind water (extract from tamarind pulp)
½ teaspoon red chili powder
½ teaspoon roasted cumin powder
½ teaspoon chaat masala
½ teaspoon black salt
Salt, to taste
Fresh coriander leaves, chopped, for garnish
Lemon wedges, for garnish

*Puris*
1 cup all-purpose flour
¼ teaspoon salt
1 tablespoon oil

Water, as needed

Oil, for deep frying

### Green Chutney

1 cup fresh coriander leaves

1 small green chili

1 small garlic clove

½ inch piece of ginger

½ teaspoon cumin seeds

Salt, to taste

Water, as needed

## Preparation

### Puris

Combine the all-purpose flour, salt, and oil in a suitable mixing bowl. Mix. Slowly pour in the water and knead the prepared dough until smooth and firm. Cover the prepared dough with some damp cloth and leave it for 20 minutes. Heat the oil in a suitable deep frying pan over medium-high heat. Divide this prepared dough into small balls and roll them out into small circles using a rolling pin. Carefully drop the rolled out dough circles into the oil and fry until golden in color on both sides. Using a slotted spoon, remove the puris from the hot oil and spread them on a (paper towel-lined) plate to drain excess oil. Set aside.

### Green Chutney

Blend together the fresh coriander leaves, green chili, garlic clove, ginger, cumin seeds, salt, and water in a suitable blender or food processor. Set aside.

### *Chotpoti*

In a suitable mixing bowl, combine the mashed chickpeas, chopped onion, chopped tomato, chopped cucumber, green chili, red chili powder, roasted cumin powder, chaat masala, black salt, and salt to taste. Mix. Add the tamarind water to the chickpea mixture and stir to combine.

To serve, place a portion of the mashed chickpea mixture in a serving bowl or plate. Drizzle some green chutney and tamarind water over the top. Garnish and serve.

# Shing Bhaja

**Preparation time:** 15 minutes
**Cook time:** 35 minutes
**Nutrition facts (per serving):** 159 Cal (9g fat, 4g protein, 4g fiber)

Shing Bhaja, also known as Masoor Dal Bora, is a popular Bengali snack made from crispy fried lentil cakes. These lentil cakes derive from ground masoor dal (red lentils) that are seasoned with spices and deep-fried until crispy.

## Ingredients (4 servings)

1 cup masoor dal (red lentils)
1 small onion, finely chopped
1 small green chili, finely chopped
½ teaspoon ginger paste
½ teaspoon cumin seeds
½ teaspoon red chili powder
½ teaspoon turmeric powder
Salt, to taste
Oil, for deep frying

## Preparation

Wash the masoor dal thoroughly and soak it in water for 3-4 hours. Drain the soaked dal and transfer it to a suitable blender or food processor. Add the chopped onion, green chili, ginger paste, cumin seeds, red chili powder, turmeric powder, and salt to the blender or food processor. Blend the prepared mixture until you get a smooth batter. Heat the oil in a suitable deep frying pan over medium-high heat. Drop spoonfuls of the lentil batter into the hot oil, making small round discs or cakes. Fry the lentil cakes until they turn golden in color and crispy on both sides. Using a slotted spoon, remove the lentil cakes from the hot oil and spread them on a (paper towel-lined) plate. Repeat this whole process with the remaining batter, frying the lentil cakes in batches.

# Chola Bhaja

**Preparation time:** 15 minutes
**Cook time:** 35 minutes
**Nutrition facts (per serving):** 203 Cal (15g fat, 7g protein, 4g fiber)

Chola Bhaja, also known as Chana Bhaja, is a popular Bengali snack made from spiced fried chickpeas. These crispy and flavorful chickpeas are seasoned with a blend of spices and deep-fried until golden.

## Ingredients (4 servings)
1 cup chickpeas (chola), soaked overnight and boiled until tender
1 small onion, finely chopped
1 small green chili, finely chopped
½ teaspoon ginger paste
½ teaspoon cumin seeds
½ teaspoon turmeric powder
½ teaspoon red chili powder
Salt, to taste
Oil, for deep frying

## Preparation
Heat the oil in a suitable deep frying pan over medium-high heat. Add the boiled chickpeas to the hot oil and cook them until golden in color and crispy. Remove them from the oil using any slotted spoon. In a separate pan, warm up a little oil and add the cumin seeds. Let them crackle. Add chopped onion, green chili, and ginger paste to the pan. Sauté until the onion turns translucent. Add the turmeric, red chili powder, and salt to taste. Sauté the spices for a minute. Add the fried

chickpeas to the pan with the spices and Mix. Turn off its heat and let the Chola Bhaja cool down slightly. Serve the crispy and spiced Chola Bhaja as a delicious Bengali snack or side dish with tea or as a topping for salads or chaats.

# Shami Kebab

**Preparation time:** 15 minutes
**Cook time:** 35 minutes
**Nutrition facts (per serving):** 232 Cal (14g fat, 10g protein, 1.3g fiber)

Shami Kebab is a popular dish in Bangladesh made with minced meat patties that are spiced with aromatic spices and deep-fried until golden.

## Ingredients (4 servings)

9 oz. minced meat (beef, lamb, or chicken)

½ cup chana dal (Bengal gram lentils), soaked in water for 1-2 hours

1 small onion, finely chopped

2-3 cloves garlic, minced

1-inch piece of ginger, minced

1-2 green chilies, finely chopped

½ teaspoon turmeric powder

½ teaspoon red chili powder

½ teaspoon garam masala powder

½ teaspoon cumin seeds

½ teaspoon coriander seeds

¼ teaspoon black peppercorns

1-2 cloves

Salt, to taste

Oil, for frying

Fresh coriander leaves, for garnish

## Preparation

In a suitable pot, add the soaked chana dal along with enough water to cover it. Cook it to a boil and cook until the dal is soft and cooked through. Drain any excess water and set aside. In a separate pan, roast the cumin seeds, coriander seeds, black peppercorns, and cloves until fragrant. Let them cool fist and then grind them into a fine powder. In a suitable mixing bowl, combine the minced meat, cooked chana dal, chopped onion, minced garlic, minced ginger, chopped green chilies, turmeric powder, red chili powder, garam masala powder, and the ground spice powder from step 2. Mix everything well. Add salt to taste and mix again.

Heat the oil in a suitable deep frying pan over medium heat. Shape the meat mixture into small patties or kebabs. Fry the kebabs in hot oil until they turn golden in color and crispy on both sides. Flip them carefully to ensure even frying. Remove the fried kebabs from the oil using any slotted spoon. Garnish the Shami Kebabs with coriander leaves. Serve hot as a delicious snack or appetizer with mint chutney, yogurt dip, or your favorite sauce.

# Samosa

**Preparation time:** 15 minutes
**Cook time:** 35 minutes
**Nutrition facts (per serving):** 142 Cal (5g fat, 6g protein, 1.2g fiber)

Samosa is a triangular-shaped snack from the Indian subcontinent, consisting of a crispy pastry shell filled with spiced potatoes, peas, onions, or meat. It's a popular street food and appetizer, often served with chutney or hot sauce for dipping.

## Ingredients (4 servings)
### Samosa Dough
1 cup all-purpose flour
¼ teaspoon salt
2 tablespoons oil
¼ cup water

### Samosa Filling
2 medium potatoes, boiled and mashed
½ cup frozen or boiled peas
½ teaspoon cumin seeds
½ teaspoon mustard seeds
½ teaspoon turmeric powder
½ teaspoon red chili powder
½ teaspoon garam masala
½ teaspoon dry mango powder (amchur)
½ teaspoon salt, or to taste
2 tablespoons oil
2 tablespoons fresh coriander leaves, chopped

Oil, for deep frying

**Preparation**
*Samosa Dough*
In a suitable mixing bowl, add the all-purpose flour, salt, and oil. Mix until the prepared mixture resembles breadcrumbs. Slowly pour in the water and knead to form a smooth and stiff dough. Cover the prepared dough with some damp cloth and leave for 20 minutes.

*Samosa Filling*
Heat the oil in a suitable pan over medium heat. Add the cumin seeds and the mustard seeds. Let them splutter. Add the mashed potatoes and peas to the pan. Mix. Stir in the turmeric powder, red chili powder, garam masala, dry mango powder, and salt. Mix and continue cooking for 2-3 minutes until the spices are well incorporated. Remove from heat and allow this filling to cool. For

*Assembling and Frying Samosas*
Divide the prepared dough into equal-sized balls and spread them into thin circles. Cut each circle in half to form semi-circles. Take one semi-circle, moisten the straight edge with water, and form a cone shape by bringing the two edges together and sealing the edges by pressing firmly. Fill the cone with a spoonful of the prepared filling, leaving some space at the top. Moisten the top edge of the cone with water and press to seal the samosa completely. Repeat this whole process with its remaining dough and filling to make all the samosas. Heat the oil in a suitable deep frying pan over medium heat. Once the oil is hot, gently slide a few samosas into the hot oil and fry them until golden and crispy. Using a slotted spoon, remove the fried samosas from the oil. Repeat the frying process with the

remaining samosas. Serve hot and crispy samosas with mint chutney, tamarind chutney, or tomato ketchup as a dipping sauce.

# Samosa Chaat

**Preparation time:** 15 minutes
**Cook time:** 35 minutes
**Nutrition facts (per serving):** 250 Cal (9.8g fat, 8g protein, 4g fiber)

Samosa Chaat is a popular fusion dish that combines the flavors of samosas, yogurt, chutneys, and spices to create a delicious and tangy street food. It's a perfect blend of crispy, savory, and spicy flavors that are sure to tantalize your taste buds.

## Ingredients (4 servings)
### Samosas
12 samosas (store-bought or homemade)
Oil, for deep frying

### Yogurt
1 cup plain yogurt
½ teaspoon salt
½ teaspoon black salt
½ teaspoon cumin powder
½ teaspoon red chili powder

### Green Chutney
1 cup fresh coriander leaves
½ cup fresh mint leaves
1 small green chili, chopped
½ inch piece of ginger, chopped
1 tablespoon lemon juice

Salt, to taste

### *Tamarind Chutney*

½ cup tamarind pulp

¼ cup jaggery or brown sugar

1 teaspoon cumin seeds

½ teaspoon red chili powder

¼ teaspoon black salt

Salt, to taste

### *Assembly*

½ cup onion, finely chopped

½ cup tomato, finely chopped

½ cup chickpeas, boiled

¼ cup nylon sev (crunchy chickpea flour noodles)

Fresh coriander leaves, for garnish

Lemon wedges, for serving

## Preparation

### *Samosas*

If using store-bought samosas, deep fry them in hot oil until crispy in color. If making homemade samosas, follow your preferred samosa recipe and deep fry them until crispy and golden in color. Set aside.

### *Yogurt*

In a suitable mixing bowl, whisk together the plain yogurt, salt, black salt, cumin powder, and red chili powder until well combined. Set aside.

### *Green Chutney*

In a suitable blender or food processor, blend together the coriander leaves, mint leaves, green chili, ginger, lemon juice, and salt to a smooth paste. Set aside.

### *Tamarind Chutney*

In a saucepan, add the tamarind pulp, jaggery or brown sugar, cumin seeds, red chili powder, black salt, and salt. Cook on low heat on a simmer, with occasional stirring, until the jaggery or sugar dissolves and the chutney thickens slightly, about 5 minutes. Remove from heat and let it cool.

### *Assembly*

Place the fried samosas on a serving plate. Drizzle the prepared yogurt over the samosas. Spoon the green chutney and tamarind chutney over the yogurt. Sprinkle the finely chopped onion and tomato over the top. Add the boiled chickpeas on top. Sprinkle nylon sev over the chaat. Garnish with coriander leaves. Serve Samosa Chaat immediately with lemon wedges on the side.

# Salads

# Kacha Kola'r Salad

**Preparation time:** 15 minutes
**Cook time:** 35 minutes
**Nutrition facts (per serving):** 222 Cal (8g fat, 9g protein, 0.8g fiber)

Kacha Kola'r Salad or Raw Banana Salad is a refreshing and nutritious salad from the Bengali cuisine, made with thinly sliced raw bananas, sliced onions, green chilies, and mustard oil.

## Ingredients (4 servings)

2 raw bananas, peeled and thinly sliced
1 small onion, thinly sliced
1-2 green chilies, finely chopped
2 tablespoons mustard oil
1 tablespoon lemon juice
½ teaspoon roasted cumin powder
½ teaspoon red chili powder
Salt, to taste
Fresh cilantro leaves, for garnish

## Preparation

Place the thinly sliced raw bananas in a suitable bowl of cold water to prevent them from turning brown. In a separate bowl, combine the sliced onions, chopped green chilies, mustard oil, lemon juice, roasted cumin powder, red chili powder, and salt. Mix to make the dressing. Drain the sliced raw bananas from the water and add them to the dressing. Toss gently to coat the bananas with the dressing. Let the salad sit for about 10 minutes to allow the flavors to meld together. Garnish the salad with fresh cilantro (coriander) leaves just before serving. Serve the Kacha Kola'r Salad as a refreshing side dish with your favorite Bangladeshi meal or as a light and healthy snack.

# Chana Chatpati

**Preparation time:** 15 minutes
**Cook time:** 35 minutes
**Nutrition facts (per serving):** 221 Cal (12g fat, 3.2g protein, 4g fiber)

Chana Chatpati is a tangy and spicy chickpea salad from the Indian subcontinent, made with boiled chickpeas, chopped onions, tomatoes, green chilies, and a blend of spices like cumin powder, chaat masala, and lemon juice. It's a popular street food and snack item, often served in paper cones or bowls.

## Ingredients (4 servings)
1 cup chickpeas (chana), boiled
1 small onion, finely chopped
1 small tomato, finely chopped
1 green chili, finely chopped
¼ cup fresh cilantro (coriander) leaves, chopped
2 tablespoons tamarind chutney
1 tablespoon mint chutney
½ teaspoon cumin powder, roasted
½ teaspoon red chili powder
Salt, to taste
Lemon wedges, for garnish

## Preparation
In a suitable bowl, combine the boiled chickpeas, chopped onion, chopped tomato, chopped green chili, and chopped cilantro. Add the tamarind chutney and the mint chutney to the bowl. Add the roasted

cumin powder, red chili powder, and salt to the bowl. Mix to coat the chickpeas and vegetables with the spices and chutneys. Let the salad sit for about 10 minutes to allow the flavors to meld together. Garnish the Chana Chatpati with lemon wedges just before serving. Serve the Chana Chatpati as a tangy and spicy chickpea salad, perfect as a refreshing side dish or a light and healthy snack.

# Cucumber Salad

**Preparation time:** 15 minutes
**Cook time:** 35 minutes
**Nutrition facts (per serving):** 221 Cal (12g fat, 3.2g protein, 4g fiber)

Bengali Cucumber Salad is a simple yet flavorful salad from the Bengali cuisine, made with thinly sliced cucumbers, sliced onions, green chilies, and a dressing of mustard oil, cumin powder, and lemon juice. It's a refreshing side dish and a perfect complement to spicy Bengali curries and rice dishes.

## Ingredients (4 servings)

2 medium cucumbers, peeled and thinly sliced
1 small red onion, thinly sliced
¼ cup fresh cilantro (coriander) leaves, chopped
2 tablespoons lemon juice
1 tablespoon olive oil
½ teaspoon sugar
Salt, to taste
Black pepper, to taste

Preparation
In a suitable bowl, combine the sliced cucumbers, sliced red onion, and chopped cilantro. In a suitable bowl, whisk together the lemon juice, olive oil, sugar, salt, and black pepper to make the dressing. Pour the dressing over the cucumber mixture in the bowl. Toss well to coat the cucumbers and onions with the dressing. Let the salad sit for about 10 minutes. Taste and adjust the seasoning with additional salt, pepper, or lemon juice, if

desired. Serve the Cucumber Salad as a refreshing side dish or a light and healthy snack.

# Beetroot Salad

**Preparation time:** 15 minutes
**Cook time:** 35 minutes
**Nutrition facts (per serving):** 211 Cal (6g fat, 5g protein, 4g fiber)

Beetroot Salad is a colorful and nutritious salad made with boiled or roasted beetroot, mixed greens, feta cheese, walnuts, and a vinaigrette dressing of olive oil and balsamic vinegar. It's a healthy and flavorful side dish that can also be served as a light lunch or dinner option.

## Ingredients (4 servings)

2 medium beets, peeled and grated
1 small red onion, thinly sliced
¼ cup crumbled feta cheese
2 tablespoons balsamic vinegar
2 tablespoons extra-virgin olive oil
1 tablespoon honey
Salt, to taste
Black pepper, to taste
Chopped fresh parsley or cilantro, for garnish (optional)

## Preparation

In a suitable bowl, combine the grated beets, sliced red onion, and crumbled feta cheese. In a suitable bowl, whisk together the balsamic vinegar, olive oil, honey, salt, and black pepper to make the dressing. Pour the dressing over the beet mixture in the bowl. Toss well to coat the ingredients with the dressing. Let the salad sit for about 10-15 minutes. Taste and adjust the seasoning with additional salt, pepper, or honey, if desired. Garnish the Beetroot Salad with chopped fresh parsley or cilantro (if using) before serving. Serve the Beetroot Salad as a colorful and nutritious side dish or as a refreshing appetizer.

# Tomato Kachumber Salad

**Preparation time:** 15 minutes
**Cook time:** 35 minutes
**Nutrition facts (per serving):** 182 Cal (1g fat, 0g protein, 1.3g fiber)

Tomato Kachumber Salad is a simple and refreshing salad from the Indian subcontinent, made with chopped tomatoes, onions, cucumbers, and coriander leaves, seasoned with salt, lemon juice, and chili powder.

## Ingredients (4 servings)

2 medium tomatoes, finely chopped
1 small red onion, finely chopped
1 small cucumber, peeled and finely chopped
1 small green chili, finely chopped (optional)
1 tablespoon freshly squeezed lemon juice
1 tablespoon fresh cilantro or mint leaves, finely chopped
½ teaspoon roasted cumin powder
Salt, to taste
Black pepper ,to taste

## Preparation

In a suitable bowl, combine the chopped tomatoes, red onion, cucumber, and green chili (if using).Add the freshly squeezed lemon juice, chopped cilantro or mint leaves, roasted cumin powder, salt, and black pepper to the bowl. Toss all the ingredients together gently to coat them with the dressing. Taste and adjust the seasoning with additional salt, black pepper, or lemon juice if desired. Refrigerate the Tomato Kachumber Salad for at least 20 minutes before serving to allow the flavors to meld together. Serve the Tomato Kachumber Salad as a refreshing and healthy side dish or as a light appetizer.

# Bhindi Salad

**Preparation time:** 15 minutes
**Cook time:** 35 minutes
**Nutrition facts (per serving):** 152 Cal (6g fat, 9g protein, 7g fiber)

Bhindi Salad or Okra Salad is a crunchy and tangy salad from the Indian subcontinent, made with sliced and sautéed okra, chopped onions, tomatoes, and green chilies, seasoned with lemon juice, chaat masala, and roasted cumin powder.

## Ingredients (4 servings)

9 oz. fresh okra (bhindi), washed and dried
1 small red onion, finely chopped
1 small tomato, finely chopped
1 small green chili, finely chopped (optional)
1 tablespoon freshly squeezed lemon juice
1 tablespoon finely chopped fresh cilantro or coriander leaves
½ teaspoon roasted cumin powder
Salt, to taste
Black pepper, to taste

## Preparation

Trim the ends of the okra and cut them into small pieces. Heat a tablespoon of oil in a suitable pan over medium heat. Add the chopped okra and sauté for 8-10 minutes until cooked and slightly crispy. Stir occasionally. Remove from heat and let the okra cool to room temperature. In a suitable bowl, combine the cooled okra, chopped red onion, chopped tomato, and green chili (if using).Add the freshly squeezed lemon juice, chopped cilantro or coriander leaves, roasted cumin powder, salt, and black pepper to the bowl. Toss all the ingredients together gently to coat them with the dressing. Refrigerate the Bhindi Salad for at least 20 minutes. Serve the Bhindi Salad as a delicious and crunchy side dish or as a refreshing appetizer.

# Lobia Salad

**Preparation time:** 15 minutes
**Cook time:** 35 minutes
**Nutrition facts (per serving):** 232 Cal (1g fat, 7g protein, 1.3g fiber)

Lobia Salad or Black Eyed Peas Salad is a healthy and delicious salad made with boiled black-eyed peas, chopped onions, tomatoes, bell peppers, and a dressing of olive oil and lemon juice. It's a perfect side dish or light meal that can be enjoyed as a vegan or vegetarian option, packed with protein and nutrients.

## Ingredients (4 servings)

1 cup black-eyed peas (Lobia), soaked overnight and cooked until tender
1 small red onion, finely chopped
1 small tomato, finely chopped
1 small cucumber, finely chopped
1 small green chili, finely chopped (optional)
1 tablespoon freshly squeezed lemon juice
1 tablespoon fresh cilantro or coriander leaves, finely chopped
½ teaspoon roasted cumin powder
Salt, to taste
Black pepper, to taste

## Preparation

Cook the soaked black-eyed peas in boiling water until tender. Drain and let them cool to room temperature. In a suitable bowl, combine the cooked black-eyed peas, chopped red onion, chopped tomato, chopped cucumber, and green chili (if using). Add the freshly squeezed lemon juice, chopped cilantro or coriander leaves, roasted cumin powder, salt, and black pepper to the bowl. Toss all the ingredients together gently to coat them with the dressing. Taste and adjust the seasoning with additional salt, black pepper, or lemon juice if desired. Refrigerate the Lobia Salad for at least 20 minutes. Serve the Lobia Salad as a healthy and protein-packed side dish or as a refreshing appetizer.

# Shakarula

**Preparation time:** 15 minutes
**Cook time:** 35 minutes
**Nutrition facts (per serving):** 257 Cal (14g fat, 19g protein, 3.4g fiber)

Shakarula or Green Mango Salad is a tangy and spicy salad from the Kashmiri cuisine, made with grated raw green mangoes, chopped onions, mint leaves, and a blend of spices like cumin powder, red chili powder, and fennel seeds.

## Ingredients (4 servings)
1 medium-sized green mango, peeled and grated
1 small red onion, finely chopped
1 small green chili, finely chopped (optional)
1 tablespoon freshly squeezed lemon juice
1 tablespoon fresh cilantro or coriander leaves, finely chopped
½ teaspoon roasted cumin powder
Salt, to taste
Black pepper, to taste

## Preparation
In a suitable bowl, combine the grated green mango, chopped red onion, and chopped green chili (if using). Add the freshly squeezed lemon juice, chopped cilantro or coriander leaves, roasted cumin powder, salt, and black pepper to the bowl. Toss all the ingredients together gently to coat them with the dressing. Taste and adjust the seasoning with additional salt, black pepper, or lemon juice, if desired. Refrigerate the Shakarula for

at least 20 minutes. Serve the Shakarula as a tangy and refreshing side dish or as a zesty appetizer.

# Soups

# Murgir Jhol

**Preparation time:** 15 minutes
**Cook time:** 35 minutes
**Nutrition facts (per serving):** 332 Cal (14g fat, 10g protein, 1.3g fiber)

Murgir Jhol or Bengali Chicken Soup is a light and flavorful soup from the Bengali cuisine, made with chicken pieces, potatoes, carrots, onions, and a blend of spices.

**Ingredients (4 servings)**
1 lb. chicken pieces, bone-in, skinless
1 medium onion, finely chopped
1 tablespoon ginger paste
1 tablespoon garlic paste
1 medium tomato, chopped
1 medium potato, peeled and cubed
2 green chili, slit
1 teaspoon cumin seeds
1 bay leaf
1 inch cinnamon stick
4 cardamom pods
4 cloves
½ teaspoon turmeric powder
½ teaspoon red chili powder
1 teaspoon coriander powder
½ teaspoon cumin powder
Salt, to taste
½ teaspoon sugar

2 tablespoons oil
4 cups water
Coriander leaves, chopped

**Preparation**

Heat the oil in a suitable pot or pressure cooker over medium heat. Add the cumin seeds, bay leaf, cinnamon stick, cardamom pods, and cloves. Sauté for a minute until fragrant. Toss in chopped onions and sauté until they turn golden in color. Add the ginger paste and the garlic paste. Cook for a minute. Add the chicken pieces and sauté for 4-5 minutes until they turn slightly golden. Stir in the turmeric powder, red chili powder, coriander powder, cumin powder, and salt. Mix. Add the chopped tomatoes and cook until soft. Add cubed potatoes and slit green chilies. Mix. Add water and sugar. Cook the soup to a boil. If using a pressure cooker, close the lid and cook for 2-3 whistles. If using a regular pot, cover and simmer for about 30-40 minutes until the chicken is cooked through and the potatoes are soft. Once the chicken is cooked, check for seasoning and adjust as needed. Garnish with chopped coriander leaves. Serve hot Murgir Jhol with steamed rice or bread of your choice. Enjoy!

# Dal Shorba

**Preparation time:** 15 minutes
**Cook time:** 35 minutes
**Nutrition facts (per serving):** 432 Cal (10g fat, 22g protein, 1.3g fiber)

Dal Shorba or Lentil Soup is a hearty and flavorful soup from the Indian subcontinent, made with a variety of lentils, vegetables, and spices, cooked in a tomato-based broth. Here's a nutritious and comforting dish that can be enjoyed as a vegetarian or vegan option, served with rice or bread, and often served during festive occasions and religious ceremonies.

**Ingredients (4 servings)**
½ cup yellow lentils (moong dal)
1 medium onion, finely chopped
2-3 garlic cloves, minced
1 inch ginger, grated
1 medium tomato, chopped
1 green chili, slit
1 teaspoon cumin seeds
½ teaspoon turmeric powder
½ teaspoon red chili powder
1 teaspoon coriander powder
½ teaspoon cumin powder
½ teaspoon garam masala
Salt, to taste
2 tablespoons oil or ghee
4 cups water
Coriander leaves, chopped

## Preparation

Wash the lentils thoroughly and soak them in water for about 30 minutes. Heat oil or ghee in a suitable pot over medium heat. Stir in the cumin seeds and let them splutter. Toss in the chopped onions and sauté until they turn golden in color. Add the minced garlic and the grated ginger. Cook for a minute. Add the chopped tomatoes and the slit green chili. Cook until the tomatoes turn soft. Add the turmeric powder, red chili, coriander and cumin powder, and salt. Mix. Drain the soaked lentils and add them to the pot. Stir well. Add water and cook the soup to a boil. Lower its heat and let the soup simmer for about 20-25 minutes until the lentils are fully cooked and have a smooth consistency. Add garam masala and stir well. Check for seasoning and adjust as needed. Garnish with chopped coriander leaves. Serve hot Dal Shorba with bread or rice of your choice. Enjoy the flavorful and nutritious Dal Shorba as a comforting soup!

# Palong Shorba

**Preparation time:** 15 minutes
**Cook time:** 35 minutes
**Nutrition facts (per serving):** 112 Cal (5g fat, 5g protein, 2g fiber)

Palong Shorba or Spinach Soup is a healthy and flavorful soup from the Indian subcontinent, made with pureed spinach, onions, garlic, and a blend of spices.

## Ingredients (4 servings)

2 cups spinach leaves, chopped
1 medium onion, finely chopped
3 garlic cloves, minced
1 inch ginger, grated
1 green chili, chopped
1 teaspoon cumin seeds
½ teaspoon turmeric powder
½ teaspoon red chili powder
1 teaspoon coriander powder
½ teaspoon cumin powder
2 tablespoons ghee or oil
4 cups water
Salt, to taste
½ teaspoon black pepper powder
1 tablespoon lemon juice

## Preparation

Heat the ghee or oil in a suitable pot over medium heat. Stir in the cumin seeds and cook for 30 seconds. Toss in the chopped onions and sauté until they turn translucent. Add the minced garlic, grated ginger, and chopped green chili. Cook for a minute. Add the turmeric, red chili, coriander, and cumin powder, and salt. Mix. Add the chopped spinach leaves and stir until they wilt down. Add water and cook the soup to a boil. Lower its heat and let the soup simmer for about 10-12 minutes until the spinach is fully cooked and soft. Using any immersion blender or a regular blender, puree this soup until smooth. Return this blended soup to the pot and add black pepper powder and lemon juice. Mix. Check for seasoning and adjust as needed. Serve hot Palong Shorba and garnish with some freshly chopped coriander leaves, if desired. Enjoy the nutritious and flavorful Palong Shorba as a comforting and healthy soup!

# Tomato Soup (Tomator Shorba)

**Preparation time:** 15 minutes
**Cook time:** 35 minutes
**Nutrition facts (per serving):** 688 Cal (35.9g fat, 36.9g protein, 2.1g fiber)

Tomator Shorba or Tomato Soup is a classic soup from the Indian subcontinent, made with fresh tomatoes, onions, garlic, and a blend of spices like cumin, coriander, and turmeric. It's a flavorful and comforting dish that can be enjoyed as a vegetarian or vegan option, served with bread or as a starter to a meal.

## Ingredients (4 servings)
3 cups ripe tomatoes, chopped
1 medium onion, finely chopped
3 garlic cloves, minced
1 inch ginger, grated
1 green chili, chopped
1 teaspoon cumin seeds
½ teaspoon turmeric powder
½ teaspoon red chili powder
1 teaspoon coriander powder
2 tablespoons ghee or oil
4 cups water
Salt, to taste
½ teaspoon black pepper powder
1 tablespoon lemon juice
Fresh coriander leaves, chopped

## Preparation

Heat the ghee or oil in a suitable pot over medium heat. Stir in the cumin seeds and sauté for 30 second. Toss in the chopped onions and sauté until they turn translucent. Add the minced garlic, grated ginger, and chopped green chili. Cook for a minute. Stir in the turmeric powder, red chili powder, coriander powder, and salt. Mix. Add the chopped tomatoes and cook for 5-6 minutes until they release their juices and turn soft. Add water and cook the soup to a boil. Lower its heat and let the soup simmer for about 10-12 minutes until the tomatoes are fully cooked and soft. Using your immersion blender or a regular blender, puree the soup until smooth. Return this blended soup to the pot and add black pepper powder and lemon juice. Mix. Check for seasoning and adjust as needed. Serve hot Tomator Shorba and garnish with freshly chopped coriander leaves, if desired. Enjoy the tangy and delicious Tomator Shorba as a comforting and flavorful tomato soup!

# Bhutte Ka Shorba

**Preparation time:** 15 minutes
**Cook time:** 35 minutes
**Nutrition facts (per serving):** 367 Cal (7.7g fat, 4.5g protein, 1g fiber)

Bhutte Ka Shorba or Corn Soup is a delicious and creamy soup from the Indian subcontinent, made with sweet corn kernels, onions, garlic, and a blend of spices. It's a comforting dish that can be enjoyed as a vegetarian or vegan option, served with bread or as a starter to a meal.

## Ingredients (4 servings)

1 cup sweet corn kernels, boiled
1 medium onion, finely chopped
3 garlic cloves, minced
1 inch ginger, grated
1 green chili, chopped
1 teaspoon cumin seeds
½ teaspoon turmeric powder
½ teaspoon red chili powder
1 teaspoon coriander powder
2 tablespoons ghee or oil
4 cups water or vegetable broth
Salt, to taste
½ teaspoon black pepper powder
¼ cup fresh cream
Fresh coriander leaves, chopped

## Preparation

Heat the ghee or oil in a suitable pot over medium heat. Stir in the cumin seeds and sauté for 30 seconds. Toss in the chopped onions and sauté until they turn translucent. Add the minced garlic, grated ginger, and chopped green chili. Cook for a minute. Stir in the turmeric powder, red chili powder, coriander powder, and salt. Mix. Add the boiled corn kernels and cook for 3-4 minutes. Add water or vegetable broth and cook the soup to a boil. Lower its heat and let the soup simmer for about 10-12 minutes, allowing the flavors to meld together. Using your immersion blender or a regular blender, puree the cooked soup until smooth. Return this blended soup to the pot and add black pepper powder and fresh cream. Mix. Check for seasoning and adjust as needed. Serve hot Bhutte Ka Shorba and garnish with freshly chopped coriander leaves, if desired. Enjoy the creamy and delicious Bhutte Ka Shorba, a comforting corn soup packed with flavors!

# Mushroom Soup
# (Mushroom Shorba)

**Preparation time:** 15 minutes

**Cook time:** 35 minutes

**Nutrition facts (per serving):** 234 Cal (7.7g fat, 8.8g protein, 4g fiber)

Mushroom Shorba or Mushroom Soup is a creamy and flavorful soup made with mushrooms, onions, garlic, and a blend of spices like thyme, oregano, and black pepper. It's a comforting meal that can be enjoyed as a vegetarian or vegan option, served with bread or as a starter to a meal.

**Ingredients (4 servings)**

2 cups mushrooms, sliced

1 medium onion, finely chopped

3 garlic cloves, minced

1 inch ginger, grated

1 green chili, chopped

1 teaspoon cumin seeds

½ teaspoon turmeric powder

½ teaspoon red chili powder

1 teaspoon coriander powder

2 tablespoons ghee or oil

4 cups water or vegetable broth

Salt, to taste

½ teaspoon black pepper powder

¼ cup fresh cream

Fresh coriander leaves, chopped

## Preparation

Heat the ghee or oil in a suitable pot over medium heat. Stir in the cumin seeds and sauté for 30 seconds. Toss in the chopped onions and sauté until they turn translucent. Add the minced garlic, grated ginger, and chopped green chili. Cook for a minute. Stir in the turmeric powder, red chili powder, coriander powder, and salt. Mix. Add sliced mushrooms and cook for 3-4 minutes. Add water or vegetable broth and cook the soup to a boil. Lower its heat and let the soup simmer for about 10-12 minutes, allowing the flavors to meld together. Using your immersion blender or a regular blender, puree the soup until smooth. Return this blended soup to the pot and add black pepper powder and fresh cream. Mix. Check for seasoning and adjust as needed. Serve hot Mushroom Shorba and garnish with freshly chopped coriander leaves, if desired. Enjoy the rich and comforting Mushroom Shorba, a delicious soup that's perfect for mushroom lovers!

# Bhapa Ilish Shorba

**Preparation time:** 15 minutes
**Cook time:** 35 minutes
**Nutrition facts (per serving):** 264 Cal (6.1g fat, 10.3 protein, 4g fiber)

Bhapa Ilish Shorba or Steamed Hilsa Fish Soup is a signature dish from the Bengali cuisine, made with Hilsa fish, mustard paste, yogurt, and a blend of spices, steamed and then cooked in a tomato-based broth. It's a flavorful and nutritious meal, often served with rice, and enjoyed as a delicacy during festive occasions and special events.

**Ingredients (4 servings)**
4 pieces hilsa fish fillets
2 tablespoons mustard paste
½ teaspoon turmeric powder
½ teaspoon green chili paste
½ teaspoon ginger paste
Salt, to taste
2 tablespoons mustard oil
½ teaspoon black cumin seeds (kalonji)
2 bay leaves
1 medium onion, finely chopped
4 garlic cloves, minced
1 medium tomato, chopped
1 teaspoon coriander powder
½ teaspoon cumin powder
½ teaspoon red chili powder
2 cups water
Fresh coriander leaves, chopped

**Preparation**

Clean and wash the Hilsa fish fillets. Pat dry with a paper towel. In a suitable mixing bowl, combine the mustard paste, turmeric powder, green chili paste, ginger paste, and salt. Mix. Add the Hilsa fish fillets to the bowl and coat them well with the mustard paste mixture. Let them marinate for 30 minutes. Heat the mustard oil in a suitable pan over medium heat. Add the black cumin seeds (kalonji) and bay leaves. Let them splutter. Add finely chopped onion and minced garlic. Sauté until the onion turns golden in color. Toss in the chopped tomatoes and cook until they turn soft. Add the coriander powder, cumin powder, and red chili powder. Mix. Add water and cook the prepared mixture to a boil.

Once the water starts boiling, lower its heat and place a steamer rack over the pan. Place the marinated Hilsa fish fillets on the steamer rack, cover the pan with a lid, and let the fish steam for about 10-12 minutes or until cooked through. Carefully remove the steamer rack with the fish fillets from the pan and set aside. Transfer the steamed fish fillets along with the broth to a serving bowl. Garnish with freshly chopped coriander leaves. Serve hot Bhapa Ilish Shorba with rice or bread of your choice. Enjoy the delightful flavors of Bhapa Ilish Shorba, a traditional Bengali fish soup that's perfect for seafood lovers!

# Narkel Shorba

**Preparation time:** 15 minutes
**Cook time:** 35 minutes
**Nutrition facts (per serving):** 473 Cal (11g fat, 36g protein, 2g fiber)

Narkel Shorba or Coconut Soup is a creamy and flavorful soup from the Indian subcontinent, made with coconut milk, onions, garlic, and a blend of spices like cumin, coriander, and turmeric. It's a comforting meal that can be enjoyed as a vegetarian or vegan option, served with bread or as a starter to a meal. The use of coconut milk gives it a rich and creamy texture.

## Ingredients (4 servings)

1 cup fresh coconut, grated
1 medium onion, finely chopped
2-3 garlic cloves, minced
1 teaspoon ginger, grated
1-2 green chili, chopped
½ teaspoon mustard seeds
½ teaspoon cumin seeds
½ teaspoon turmeric powder
Salt, to taste
1 tablespoon vegetable oil
2 cups water
Fresh coriander leaves, chopped

## Preparation

Heat the vegetable oil in a suitable pan over medium heat. Add the mustard seeds and cumin seeds. Let them splutter. Add the finely chopped onion, minced garlic, grated ginger, and chopped green chili. Sauté until the onion turns translucent. Add the grated coconut and cook for 3-4 minutes until the coconut turns slightly golden in color. Add the turmeric powder and salt. Mix. Add water and cook the prepared mixture to a boil. Once the prepared mixture starts boiling, lower its heat and Cook it on a simmer for about 10-15 minutes until the flavors meld together and the soup thickens slightly. Remove from heat and let the soup cool for a few minutes. Use your immersion blender or a regular blender to blend the soup until smooth. Transfer the blended soup back to the pan and reheat, if needed. Serve hot Narkel Shorba in soup bowls. Garnish with freshly chopped coriander leaves. Enjoy the creamy and flavorful Narkel Shorba as a comforting appetizer or a light meal.

# Morog Polao Shorba

**Preparation time:** 15 minutes
**Cook time:** 35 minutes
**Nutrition facts (per serving):** 403 Cal (23g fat, 17g protein, 2g fiber)

Morog Polao Shorba or Chicken Pilaf Soup is a hearty and flavorful soup from the Bengali cuisine, made with chicken, aromatic spices, and rice, cooked in a tomato-based broth. It's a delicious and nourishing dish that can be enjoyed as an entrée or a starter, served with bread or rice, and often served during festive occasions and special events.

## Ingredients (4 servings)
1 lb. chicken, bone-in pieces
1 cup basmati rice, rinsed
1 large onion, thinly sliced
1 tablespoon ginger-garlic paste
1 medium tomato, chopped
¼ cup yogurt
½ teaspoon turmeric powder
½ teaspoon red chili powder
½ teaspoon cumin seeds
1 inch cinnamon stick
2-3 cardamom pods
2-3 cloves
2 bay leaves
2 tablespoons ghee (clarified butter)
Salt, to taste
Coriander leaves, chopped

## Preparation

Heat the ghee in a suitable pot or pan over medium heat. Add the cumin seeds, cinnamon stick, cardamom pods, cloves, and bay leaves. Sauté for a minute until fragrant. Add the thinly sliced onion and sauté until golden. Stir in the ginger-garlic paste and sauté for another minute. Add the chicken pieces and cook until they turn slightly golden on all sides. Add the chopped tomatoes, turmeric powder, salt and red chili powder. Continue cooking until the tomatoes turn soft. Add the yogurt and cook for 2-3 minutes until the chicken is coated with the yogurt and the spices are well blended. Add the soaked and drained basmati rice to the pot and stir well. Add 4-5 cups of water, cover the pot with a lid, and let the soup come to a boil. Once the soup comes to a boil, lower its heat and Cook it on a simmer for about 20 minutes until the rice and chicken are cooked through and the flavors meld together. Check for seasoning and adjust salt and spices as needed. Garnish with freshly chopped coriander leaves. Serve hot Morog Polao Shorba in soup bowls. Enjoy the aromatic and flavorful chicken pilaf soup as a delicious meal on its own or with some bread or naan on the side.

# Main dishes

# Hilsa Bhapa

**Preparation time:** 15 minutes
**Cook time:** 35 minutes
**Nutrition facts (per serving):** 467 Cal (29g fat, 28g protein, 3g fiber)

Hilsa Bhapa, also known as Steamed Hilsa Fish, is a popular Bengali dish that features hilsa fish marinated in mustard paste, wrapped in banana leaves, and steamed to perfection.

## Ingredients (4 servings)
6 pieces of hilsa fish fillets
½ cup mustard seeds
3 green chilies, slit lengthwise
½ cup yogurt
2 tablespoon mustard oil
½ teaspoon turmeric powder
Salt, to taste
Banana leaves, cut into square pieces, for wrapping

## Preparation
Soak the mustard seeds in water for about 30 minutes. Then, drain the water and grind the mustard seeds into a smooth paste using a mortar and pestle or a food processor. In a suitable bowl, mix together the mustard paste, yogurt, mustard oil, turmeric powder, and salt to form a marinade. Clean and pat dry the hilsa fish fillets. Rub the fish fillets with the mustard marinade, ensuring that the fish is well-coated with the marinade. Take a piece of banana leaf and lightly heat it over an open flame or in a hot pan to make it pliable. Place a fish fillet coated with the mustard marinade on

the banana leaf. Add a slit green chili on top. Fold the banana leaf to wrap the fish fillet securely, forming a neat parcel. Repeat this whole process with the remaining fish fillets and banana leaves. Place the banana leaf-wrapped fish parcels in a steamer or a suitable pan with a steamer rack. Steam the fish parcels for 10-15 minutes. Carefully unwrap the banana leaves and transfer the steamed fish fillets to a serving plate. Serve hot with steamed rice or parboiled rice, and enjoy the delicious Hilsa Bhapa - Steamed Hilsa Fish!

# Meacher Jhol

**Preparation time:** 15 minutes
**Cook time:** 35 minutes
**Nutrition facts (per serving):** 408 Cal (6.2g fat, 34g protein, 4g fiber)

Maacher Jhol, also known as Bengali Fish Curry, is a popular and traditional fish curry from Bengal, a region in Eastern India. It's a pretty simple yet flavorful dish that features fish cooked in a light and spicy broth made with spices, tomatoes, and sometimes vegetables. It's usually served with steamed rice or parboiled rice.

**Ingredients (4 servings)**
1 lb. fish (Rohu, Katla, or Hilsa), cleaned and cut into pieces
1 medium-sized onion, finely chopped
2 medium-sized tomatoes, chopped
3 green chilies, slit lengthwise
½ inch piece of ginger, grated
3 cloves of garlic, minced
½ teaspoon turmeric powder
½ teaspoon red chili powder
½ teaspoon cumin seeds
½ teaspoon mustard seeds
½ teaspoon cumin powder
½ teaspoon coriander powder
½ teaspoon garam masala powder
2 tablespoon mustard oil
Fresh coriander leaves, for garnish
Salt, to taste

**Preparation**

Heat the mustard oil in a suitable pan or kadai over medium heat. Stir the cumin seeds and mustard seeds, and cook for 30 seconds. Toss in the chopped onions and sauté until they turn translucent. Add the grated ginger and minced garlic, and sauté for another minute. Add the chopped tomatoes and slit green chilies, and cook until the tomatoes are soft. Stir in the turmeric powder, red chili powder, cumin powder, coriander powder, and salt. Mix. Add the fish pieces to the pan and gently coat them with the spice mixture. Add enough water to cover the fish pieces and cook the curry to a boil. Reduce its heat to low and let the curry simmer for about 10-12 minutes, or until the fish is cooked through. Sprinkle garam masala powder and fresh coriander leaves over the curry, and turn off the heat. Serve hot with steamed rice or parboiled rice, and enjoy the delicious Maacher Jhol - Bengali Fish Curry!

# Fish in Mustard Sauce (Pabda Shorshe)

**Preparation time:** 15 minutes
**Cook time:** 35 minutes
**Nutrition facts (per serving):** 421 Cal (16g fat, 29g protein, 0g fiber)

Pabda Shorshe, or Pabda Fish in Mustard Sauce, is a popular Bengali fish curry that features Pabda fish cooked in a flavorful mustard sauce. The tangy and spicy mustard sauce pairs perfectly with the tender and succulent Pabda fish, making it a delicious and aromatic dish.

## Ingredients (4 servings)
1 lb. Pabda fish, cleaned and washed
2 tablespoons mustard seeds
3 green chilies, slit lengthwise
½ teaspoon turmeric powder
½ teaspoon red chili powder
½ teaspoon cumin seeds
½ teaspoon nigella seeds (kalonji)
½ teaspoon fenugreek seeds (methi)
½ cup mustard oil
Salt, to taste
Fresh coriander leaves, for garnish

## Preparation
Soak the mustard seeds in water for about 30 minutes. Drain the water and grind the mustard seeds along with green chilies to a smooth paste. You can add a little water if needed. Heat the mustard oil in a suitable pan

or kadai over medium heat. Add the cumin seeds, nigella seeds, and fenugreek seeds, and let them splutter. Add the ground mustard paste, turmeric powder, red chili powder, and salt. Mix. Add the fish pieces to the pan and gently coat them with the mustard sauce. Add enough water to cover the fish pieces and cook the curry to a boil. Reduce its heat to low and let the curry simmer for about 10-12 minutes. Turn off its heat and let the curry rest for a few minutes. Garnish with coriander leaves. Serve hot with steamed rice or parboiled rice, and enjoy the delicious Pabda Shorshe - Pabda Fish in Mustard Sauce!

# Fish in Yogurt Curry
# (Doi Maach)

**Preparation time:** 15 minutes
**Cook time:** 35 minutes
**Nutrition facts (per serving):** 384 Cal (4.7g fat, 20g protein, 1.7g fiber)

Doi Maach, or Fish in Yogurt Curry, is a popular Bengali dish where fish is cooked in a creamy and tangy yogurt-based curry. The use of yogurt gives this curry a rich and luscious texture, while the spices and flavors make it a delicious and comforting dish.

## Ingredients (4 servings)
1 lb. fish pieces (such as Rohu, Katla, or Hilsa)
½ cup plain yogurt (curd)
½ teaspoon turmeric powder
½ teaspoon red chili powder
½ teaspoon cumin seeds
½ teaspoon mustard seeds
½ teaspoon nigella seeds (kalonji)
½ teaspoon fenugreek seeds (methi)
1 bay leaf
2-3 green chilies, slit lengthwise
2 tablespoon mustard oil
Salt, to taste
Fresh coriander leaves, for garnish

**Preparation**

Marinate the fish pieces with salt and turmeric powder and let them sit for 10-15 minutes. In a suitable bowl, whisk the yogurt until smooth. Heat mustard oil in a suitable pan or kadai over medium heat. Add the cumin seeds, mustard seeds, nigella seeds, fenugreek seeds, and bay leaf. Let them splutter. Add the marinated fish pieces to the pan and fry them until lightly golden on both sides. Remove and keep aside. In the same pan, add more mustard oil if needed. Add the green chilies and sauté for a minute. Lower its heat and add turmeric powder and red chili powder. Mix. Add the whisked yogurt to the pan and cook on low heat, stirring constantly to avoid curdling. Add salt and continue to cook for a few more minutes until the yogurt thickens. Add the fried fish pieces back to the pan and gently stir to coat them with the yogurt curry. Cover the pan and cook on a simmer on low heat for 8-10 minutes. Turn off its heat and let the curry rest for a few minutes. Garnish with coriander leaves. Serve hot with steamed rice or parboiled rice, and enjoy the creamy and tangy Doi Maach - Fish in Yogurt Curry!

# Prawn Curry with Coconut Milk (Chingri Malai Curry)

**Preparation time:** 15 minutes
**Cook time:** 35 minutes
**Nutrition facts (per serving):** 449 Cal (3.6g fat, 17g protein, 5.4g fiber)

Chingri Malai Curry, or Prawn Curry with Coconut Milk, is a popular Bengali dish that features succulent prawns cooked in a creamy and aromatic curry made with coconut milk. The flavors of the prawns and the richness of the coconut milk come together to create a delicious and comforting curry.

**Ingredients (4 servings)**
1 lb. prawns, cleaned and deveined
½ cup coconut milk
1 medium-sized onion, finely chopped
1 medium-sized tomato, finely chopped
2-3 green chilies, slit lengthwise
½ teaspoon turmeric powder
½ teaspoon red chili powder
½ teaspoon cumin seeds
½ teaspoon ginger paste
½ teaspoon garlic paste
½ teaspoon garam masala powder
½ teaspoon sugar
2 tablespoons oil or ghee (clarified butter)
Salt, to taste
Fresh coriander leaves, for garnish

**Preparation**

Heat the oil or ghee in a suitable pan or kadai over medium heat. Add the cumin seeds and let them splutter. Add chopped onions and sauté until golden. Add the ginger paste and the garlic paste. Sauté for a minute. Toss in the chopped tomatoes and cook until they turn soft and mushy. Add the turmeric powder, red chili powder, and sugar. Mix. Add the cleaned and deveined prawns to the pan and continue cooking for 2-3 minutes, or until they turn pink and opaque. Stir the coconut milk to the pan and cook it to a gentle boil. Lower its heat and let the curry simmer for 5-7 minutes, or until the prawns are cooked through and the flavors meld together. Stir in garam masala powder and salt to taste. Mix. Turn off its heat and let the curry rest for a few minutes. Garnish with coriander leaves. Serve warm.

# Steamed Prawns (Bhapa Chingri)

**Preparation time:** 15 minutes
**Cook time:** 35 minutes
**Nutrition facts (per serving):** 372 Cal (29g fat, 21g protein, 1.4g fiber)

Bhapa Chingri, or Steamed Prawns, is a traditional Bengali dish that features prawns marinated in a spiced yogurt mixture and then steamed to perfection. The steaming process helps to lock in the flavors of the marinade, resulting in a delicious and aromatic dish.

## Ingredients (4 servings)

1 lb. prawns, cleaned and deveined
½ cup plain yogurt
½ teaspoon turmeric powder
½ teaspoon red chili powder
½ teaspoon cumin powder
½ teaspoon coriander powder
½ teaspoon mustard oil
½ teaspoon ginger paste
½ teaspoon garlic paste
½ teaspoon sugar
Salt, to taste
Fresh coriander leaves, for garnish

## Preparation

In a suitable mixing bowl, combine the plain yogurt, turmeric powder, red chili powder, cumin powder, coriander powder, mustard oil, ginger paste, garlic paste, sugar, and salt. Mix to form a smooth marinade. Add the cleaned and deveined prawns to the marinade and coat them well with the prepared mixture. Leave the prawns to marinate for at least 30 minutes, or refrigerate for a few hours for better flavor infusion. After marination, transfer the prawns along with the marinade to a heatproof dish or a steaming tray. Prepare a steamer with water and cook it to a boil. Place the dish or tray with prawns in the steamer and steam on medium heat for 10-12 minutes, or until the prawns are cooked through and turn pink. Carefully remove the dish or tray from the steamer and garnish with coriander leaves. Serve hot with steamed rice or as a side dish, and enjoy the flavorful and tender Bhapa Chingri - Steamed Prawns!

# Rohu Fish Curry (Rui Macher Kalia)

**Preparation time:** 15 minutes
**Cook time:** 35 minutes
**Nutrition facts (per serving):** 519 Cal (24g fat, 24g protein, 14g fiber)

Rui Macher Kalia, or Rohu Fish Curry, is a popular Bengali fish dish that's known for its rich and aromatic flavors. It's typically made with marinated pieces of Rohu fish cooked in a spicy and tangy gravy.

**Ingredients (4 servings)**
1 lb. Rohu or similar fish pieces
½ cup plain yogurt
2 onions, finely chopped
2 tomatoes, chopped
½ teaspoon turmeric powder
½ teaspoon red chili powder
1 teaspoon cumin powder
1 teaspoon coriander powder
½ teaspoon ginger paste
½ teaspoon garlic paste
½ teaspoon sugar
½ teaspoon garam masala powder
2 tablespoon mustard oil
Fresh coriander leaves, for garnish
Salt, to taste

## *Marination*

½ teaspoon turmeric powder

½ teaspoon red chili powder

½ teaspoon salt

## Preparation

Wash the Rohu fish pieces thoroughly and marinate them with turmeric powder, red chili powder, and salt. Let them marinate for 20 minutes. Heat mustard oil in a suitable deep pan or kadai over medium heat. Add the marinated fish pieces and fry them until they turn golden in color on both sides. Remove the fish pieces and keep aside. In that same pan, add more oil if needed. Stir in the chopped onions and sauté until they turn golden in color. Add the ginger paste, garlic paste, turmeric powder, red chili powder, cumin powder, coriander powder, and salt. Stir and cook the spices for a minute or until the raw smell goes away. Toss in the chopped tomatoes and cook until they become soft and mushy. Add the plain yogurt and the sugar. Mix and cook for 2-3 minutes. Add fried fish pieces to the gravy and gently coat them with the spices. Be careful not to break the fish pieces. Add water if needed. Cover this pan and let the curry simmer for 10-15 minutes. Garnish with garam masala powder and garnish with coriander leaves. Serve hot with steamed rice or paratha.

# Mustard Fish Curry
# (Shorshe Bata Diye Macher Jhal)

**Preparation time:** 15 minutes
**Cook time:** 35 minutes
**Nutrition facts (per serving):** 109 Cal (4g fat, 29.5g protein, 3g fiber)

Shorshe Bata Diye Macher Jhal, or Mustard Fish Curry, is a popular Bengali fish dish known for its tangy and pungent flavors. It's typically made with a mustard paste that adds a unique and delicious taste to the fish curry.

**Ingredients (4 servings)**
1 lb. fish fillets (rohu, katla or hilsa)
2 tablespoon mustard seeds
1 tablespoon mustard oil
2 green chilies, chopped
1 onion, finely chopped
½ teaspoon turmeric powder
½ teaspoon red chili powder
½ teaspoon nigella seeds (kalonji)
½ teaspoon cumin seeds
½ teaspoon ginger paste
½ teaspoon garlic paste
½ teaspoon sugar
Salt, to taste
Fresh coriander leaves, for garnish

**Preparation**

Soak the mustard seeds in water for 30 minutes. After soaking, drain the water and make a fine paste of the mustard seeds using a grinder or mortar and pestle. You can adjust the amount of water while grinding to achieve the desired consistency of the mustard paste. Heat the mustard oil in a suitable pan over medium heat. Add the nigella seeds (kalonji) and the cumin seeds. Let them splutter. Add the chopped onions and the green chilies. Sauté until the onions turn translucent. Add the ginger paste, garlic paste, turmeric powder, red chili powder, and salt. Stir and cook the spices for a minute or until the raw smell goes away. Add the mustard paste and sugar. Mix and cook for 2-3 minutes. Add fish fillets to the pan and gently coat them with the mustard paste. Be careful not to break the fish fillets. Add water if needed. Cover the pan and cook the curry simmer for 10-15 minutes. Garnish with coriander leaves. Serve hot with steamed rice or paratha, and enjoy the tangy and pungent flavors of Shorshe Bata Diye Macher Jhal - Mustard Fish Curry!

# Fish Roe Fritters
# (Macher Dimer Bora)

**Preparation time:** 15 minutes

**Cook time:** 35 minutes

**Nutrition facts (per serving):** 236 Cal (13.8g fat,18g protein, 1.7g fiber)

Macher Dimer Bora, or Fish Roe Fritters, is a popular Bengali dish made from fish roe (fish eggs) that are deep-fried to create crispy and flavorful fritters. It's a delicious and unique way to enjoy fish eggs as a snack or appetizer.

## Ingredients (4 servings)

8 oz. fish roe (hilsa or rohu)

1 onion, finely chopped

2 green chilies, finely chopped

½ teaspoon turmeric powder

½ teaspoon red chili powder

½ teaspoon cumin seeds

½ teaspoon ginger paste

½ teaspoon garlic paste

1 tablespoon besan (gram flour)

1 tablespoon rice flour

1 tablespoon coriander leaves, chopped

Salt, to taste

Oil, for deep frying

**Preparation**

Wash the fish roe thoroughly under running water to remove any impurities. In a suitable mixing bowl, add the fish roe, chopped onions, green chilies, turmeric powder, red chili powder, cumin seeds, ginger paste, garlic paste, besan, rice flour, chopped coriander leaves, and salt. Mix to form a thick batter-like consistency. Heat oil in a suitable deep frying pan over medium-high heat. Using a spoon or your fingers, drop spoonfuls of the fish roe batter into the hot oil and fry until golden and crispy. Remove the fried fritters using any slotted spoon. Serve hot as a snack or appetizer with your favorite dipping sauce or chutney. Enjoy the crispy and flavorful Macher Dimer Bora - Fish Roe Fritters as a delicious Bengali delicacy!

# Paturi

**Preparation time:** 15 minutes
**Cook time:** 35 minutes
**Nutrition facts (per serving):** 314 Cal (17g fat, 4g protein, 1g fiber)

Paturi is a popular Bengali dish made by marinating fish fillets in a flavorful spice mixture, wrapping them in banana leaves, and then steaming or grilling them. The banana leaves impart a unique aroma and flavor to the fish, making it a delicious and aromatic dish.

**Ingredients (4 servings)**
1 lb. fish fillets (such as bhetki, hilsa, or rohu)
½ cup mustard paste
¼ cup coconut, grated
2 tablespoon poppy seeds
2 tablespoon yogurt
1 tablespoon mustard oil
1 tablespoon ginger paste
1 tablespoon garlic paste
2 green chilies, finely chopped
½ teaspoon turmeric powder
½ teaspoon red chili powder
½ teaspoon sugar
Salt, to taste
Banana leaves, cut into 8 x 8-inch squares, for wrapping
Cooking twine, for tying the banana leaves

**Preparation**

In a suitable mixing bowl, add the mustard paste, grated coconut, poppy seeds, yogurt, mustard oil, ginger paste, garlic paste, green chilies, turmeric powder, red chili powder, sugar, and salt. Mix to form a smooth marinade. Coat the fish fillets with the marinade and let them marinate for almost 1 hour in the refrigerator. Take a banana leaf square and lightly heat it over a gas flame or in a hot pan to make it pliable. Place a marinated fish fillet in the center of the banana leaf square and fold the leaf to wrap the fish, securing it with cooking twine. Repeat this whole process with the remaining fish fillets and banana leaves. Steam the wrapped fish in a steamer or grill them on a barbecue for about 10-15 minutes until the fish is well-cooked. Carefully remove the fish parcels from the steamer or grill and let them cool slightly. Unwrap the banana leaves and discard them before serving. Serve the aromatic and flavorful Paturi hot with steamed rice or as part of a Bengali meal. Enjoy the delicious and unique flavors of Paturi - Fish Wrapped in Banana Leaf!

# Kosha Mangsho

**Preparation time:** 15 minutes
**Cook time:** 35 minutes
**Nutrition facts (per serving):** 428 Cal (17g fat, 57g protein, 8g fiber)

Kosha Mangsho is a famous Bengali slow-cooked mutton stew, prepared by cooking tender mutton pieces in a blend of aromatic spices like coriander, cumin, and garam masala, with onions, ginger, garlic, and tomatoes until cooked to perfection. It's a rich and flavorful dish, often served with rice or bread, and enjoyed during festive occasions and special events.

## Ingredients (4 servings)
1 lb. mutton (goat meat), cut into pieces
4 onions, thinly sliced
2 tomatoes, chopped
2 potatoes, peeled and cut into cubes
3 green chilies, slit
1 tablespoon ginger paste
1 tablespoon garlic paste
½ teaspoon turmeric powder
1 teaspoon red chili powder
1 teaspoon cumin powder
1 teaspoon coriander powder
½ teaspoon garam masala powder
½ teaspoon sugar
½ teaspoon cumin seeds
3 whole dry red chilies

3 tablespoons mustard oil

Salt, to taste

Coriander leaves, for garnish

## Preparation

Heat the mustard oil in a heavy-bottomed pan or kadai over medium heat. Add the cumin seeds and the whole dry red chilies. Let them splutter. Add the thinly sliced onions and sauté until they turn golden in color. Add the ginger paste and the garlic paste. Cook for 2-3 minutes. Fold in the chopped tomatoes and cook until they turn soft and mushy. Add the mutton pieces and cook on high heat for a few minutes until they start to change color. Reduce its heat to low and add turmeric, red chili, cumin and coriander powder, and salt. Mix. Cover and continue cooking on low heat for about 30-40 minutes or until the mutton is almost cooked, with occasional stirring to prevent burning. Add the cubed potatoes and green chilies. Continue cooking for 10-15 minutes until the potatoes are cooked through and the mutton is tender. Add garam masala powder and sugar. Mix. Increase its heat to high and cook for 2-3 more minutes until it thickens and the oil separates. Garnish with chopped coriander leaves and remove from heat. Serve hot with steamed rice or paratha.

# Niramish Begun Bhaja Diye Tetor Dal

**Preparation time:** 15 minutes
**Cook time:** 35 minutes
**Nutrition facts (per serving):** 442 Cal (37g fat, 11g protein, 0g fiber)

Niramish Begun Bhaja Diye Tetor Dal is a traditional Bengali stew made with lentils, bitter gourd, and eggplant, flavored with a mix of aromatic spices like cumin, coriander, and turmeric, and garnished with fried eggplant slices. It's a healthy and flavorful vegetarian dish, often served with rice or bread, and enjoyed as a comfort food by Bengalis.

## Ingredients (4 servings)
½ cup tetor dal (bitter gourd lentils), soaked in water for 30 minutes
1 small bitter gourd (karela), thinly sliced
1 small eggplant (baingan), cut into small cubes
1 tomato, chopped
1 tablespoon mustard oil
½ teaspoon cumin seeds
½ teaspoon turmeric powder
½ teaspoon red chili powder
½ teaspoon cumin powder
½ teaspoon coriander powder
½ teaspoon garam masala powder
½ teaspoon sugar
Salt, to taste
Coriander leaves, for garnish

## Tempering (Tadka)

1 tablespoon ghee

½ teaspoon cumin seeds

3 dry red chilies

1 pinch of Asafoetida (Hing)

## Preparation

Heat the mustard oil in a suitable pan or kadai over medium heat. Add the cumin seeds and let them splutter. Add the thinly sliced bitter gourd and cubed eggplant. Sauté them for a few minutes until they start to turn golden in color. Stir in the chopped tomatoes and cook until they turn soft and mushy. Drain the soaked tetor dal and add it to the pan. Mix. Add the turmeric powder, red chili powder, cumin powder, coriander powder, and salt. Mix. Add enough water to cover the added lentils and vegetables. Cook to a boil. Reduce its heat to low and Cook it on a simmer for about 20-25 minutes. In a separate small pan, heat ghee over low heat for the tempering. Add the cumin seeds, dry red chilies, and Asafoetida. Let them splutter. Pour the tempering over the stew and Mix. Add the garam masala powder and sugar. Mix. Simmer for a few more minutes to let the flavors meld together. Garnish with chopped coriander leaves and remove from heat. Serve hot with steamed rice or roti. Enjoy the delicious Bengali Niramish Begun Bhaja Diye Tetor Dal - bitter gourd and eggplant stew with lentils!

# Bhoger Khichuri

**Preparation time:** 15 minutes
**Cook time:** 35 minutes
**Nutrition facts (per serving):** 295 Cal (28g fat, 3g protein, 2g fiber)

Bhoger Khichuri is a popular Bengali dish prepared with rice, yellow moong dal, and a variety of vegetables like potatoes, cauliflower, and peas, cooked in a blend of aromatic spices and ghee (clarified butter). It's a comforting and nourishing dish often served during religious ceremonies or as a community meal during festivals, and is enjoyed with accompaniments like papadum and chutney.

## Ingredients (4 servings)
1 cup basmati rice, rinsed
½ cup yellow moong dal (split yellow lentils), rinsed
1 medium potato, peeled and diced
1 small carrot, peeled and diced
1 small cauliflower, florets separated
½ cup green peas
½ teaspoon turmeric powder
½ teaspoon cumin seeds
½ teaspoon ginger paste
½ teaspoon cumin powder
½ teaspoon coriander powder
½ teaspoon red chili powder
½ teaspoon garam masala powder
½ teaspoon sugar
Salt, to taste

2 tablespoons ghee

1 bay leaf

3 whole cloves

3 whole cardamom pods

1 small cinnamon stick

1 small onion, finely chopped

3 green chilies, slit lengthwise

Coriander leaves, for garnish

Water, as needed

## Preparation

Warm up the ghee in a pressure cooker or a heavy-bottomed pot over medium heat. Add the cumin seeds, bay leaf, cloves, cardamom pods, and cinnamon stick. Let them splutter and release their aroma. Add the finely chopped onion and slit green chilies. Sauté until the onions turn golden in color. Add the ginger paste and sauté for another minute. Add the diced potato, carrot, cauliflower florets, and green peas. Sauté for a few minutes. Add the turmeric powder, cumin powder, coriander powder, red chili powder, garam masala powder, sugar, and salt. Mix. Add the soaked and drained rice and moong dal. Mix to coat the rice and dal with the spices. Pour in enough water to cover the added rice and dal by about 2 inches. Cook to a boil. If using a pressure cooker, cover and pressure cook for 2 whistles on medium heat. If using a pot, cover and cook on low heat until the rice and dal are cooked through and tender, with occasional stirring to prevent sticking to the bottom. Once the khichuri is cooked, leave for a few minutes before opening the pressure cooker or pot. Garnish with coriander leaves and serve hot.

# Mochar Ghonto

**Preparation time:** 15 minutes
**Cook time:** 35 minutes
**Nutrition facts (per serving):** 343 Cal (23g fat, 13g protein, 0.6g fiber)

Mochar Ghonto is a traditional Bengali vegetarian dish prepared with banana blossoms, lentils, and a blend of aromatic spices like cumin, coriander, and turmeric. Here's a healthy and flavorful stew often served with rice or bread, and enjoyed as a comfort food by Bengalis.

## Ingredients (4 servings)
1 medium-sized banana blossom (mochar)
½ cup chana dal (Bengal gram lentils)
1 potato, peeled and diced
½ cup coconut, grated
½ teaspoon turmeric powder
½ teaspoon red chili powder
½ teaspoon cumin seeds
½ teaspoon mustard seeds
3 dry red chilies
1 bay leaf
1 cinnamon stick
3 cardamom pods
4 cloves
½ teaspoon ginger paste
½ teaspoon garlic paste
2 tablespoons oil
Salt, to taste

Sugar, to taste

Coriander leaves, for garnishing

## Preparation

### *Banana Blossom*

Peel off the outer purple layers of the banana blossom until you reach the light yellow or white part. Discard the outer layers and chop the inner part finely. Soak the chopped banana blossom in water with a pinch of turmeric powder to prevent oxidation and set aside for 20 minutes.

### *Lentils*

Wash and rinse the chana dal (Bengal gram lentils) under running water. In a pot, add the chana dal with enough water to cover it, along with ¼ teaspoon turmeric powder and a pinch of salt. Cook it to a boil and then reduce its heat to low and Cook it on a simmer until the lentils are cooked and softened. Drain any excess water and set aside. Heat the oil in a suitable deep pan or kadai over medium heat. Add the cumin seeds, mustard seeds, dry red chilies, bay leaf, cinnamon stick, cardamom pods, and cloves. Let them splutter and release their aroma.

Add the diced potato to the pan and sauté for 2-3 minutes until it turns slightly golden. Add the ginger paste and the garlic paste to the pan and sauté for another minute. Add the soaked and chopped banana blossom to the pan and Mix. Cook for 5-6 minutes until the banana blossom softens. Stir in turmeric powder, red chili powder, and salt to taste. Mix and keep cooking for 2-3 minutes. Add the cooked chana dal (lentils) to the pan and mix with the banana blossom. Add grated coconut and sugar to taste. Mix and continue cooking for 2-3 minutes. Garnish with chopped coriander leaves and remove from heat.

# Chhanar Dalna

**Preparation time:** 15 minutes
**Cook time:** 35 minutes
**Nutrition facts (per serving):** 478 Cal (26g fat, 24g protein, 2g fiber)

Chhanar Dalna is a popular Bengali vegetarian dish prepared with cottage cheese, potatoes, and a variety of vegetables like peas, carrots, and cauliflower, cooked in a blend of aromatic spices like cumin, coriander, and garam masala.

## Ingredients (4 Servings)
### Paneer (Cottage Cheese)
1 liter milk
2-3 tablespoons lemon juice or vinegar

## Chhanar Dalna
8 oz. paneer (cottage cheese), cut into cubes
1 medium-sized potato, peeled and diced
½ cup green peas
½ cup carrots, diced
½ cup cauliflower florets
½ cup tomato puree
½ teaspoon turmeric powder
½ teaspoon red chili powder
½ teaspoon cumin seeds
½ teaspoon mustard seeds
3 dry red chilies
1 bay leaf

1 cinnamon stick

3 cardamom pods

4 cloves

½ teaspoon ginger paste

½ teaspoon garlic paste

2 tablespoons oil

Salt, to taste

Sugar, to taste

Coriander leaves, for garnishing

## Preparation
### Paneer (Cottage Cheese)

Heat the milk in a suitable pot and cook it to a boil. Once the milk starts boiling, add the lemon juice or vinegar and stir gently. The milk will curdle, and you will see the whey (greenish liquid) separating from the curdled milk (paneer). Turn off its heat and strain the curdled milk using a muslin cloth or cheesecloth. Rinse the paneer under cold water to remove any lemon juice or vinegar residue. Squeeze out excess water and hang the paneer in the cloth for about 30 minutes to drain the whey completely. Once the paneer is drained, spread it on a clean flat surface and press it with a heavy object for about 1 hour to set it. After 1 hour, cut the paneer into cubes and set aside.

### Chhanar Dalna

Heat the oil in a suitable deep pan or kadai over medium heat. Add the cumin seeds, mustard seeds, dry red chilies, bay leaf, cinnamon stick, cardamom pods, and cloves. Let them splutter and release their aroma. Add the diced potatoes to the pan and sauté for 2-3 minutes until they turn slightly golden. Add the ginger paste and the garlic paste to the pan and sauté for another minute. Stir in the turmeric powder, red chili powder, and salt to taste. Mix. Pour the tomato puree into the pan and cook for 2-3 minutes until well incorporated with the spices. Add the green peas, diced carrots, and cauliflower florets to the pan. Mix. Add ½ cup of water to the pan, cover and cook on low heat for 5-6 minutes until the vegetables are partially cooked. Add the paneer (cottage cheese) cubes to the pan and gently mix them with the vegetables. Be careful not to break the paneer cubes. Add sugar to taste and Continue cooking for 2-3 minutes until the stew thickens and the paneer absorbs the flavors. Garnish with chopped coriander leaves and remove from heat.

# Aloo Potol Posto

**Preparation time:** 15 minutes
**Cook time:** 35 minutes
**Nutrition facts (per serving):** 338 Cal (10g fat, 33g protein, 3g fiber)

Aloo Potol Posto is a traditional Bengali vegetarian dish made with pointed gourd, potatoes, and a paste of poppy seeds, mustard oil, and green chilies, flavored with aromatic spices like cumin and turmeric.

## Ingredients (4 servings)
8 pointed gourds (potol), peeled and slit lengthwise
2 medium-sized potatoes, peeled and diced
3 tablespoons poppy seeds (posto)
2 green chilies, slit lengthwise
½ teaspoon turmeric powder
½ teaspoon red chili powder
½ teaspoon cumin seeds
½ teaspoon mustard seeds
3 dry red chilies
1 bay leaf
1 cinnamon stick
3 cardamom pods
4 cloves
½ teaspoon ginger paste
½ teaspoon garlic paste
2 tablespoons mustard oil (or any other cooking oil)
Salt, to taste
Sugar, to taste
Coriander leaves, for garnishing

## Preparation

Soak the poppy seeds in warm water for about 30 minutes. Drain the water and grind the poppy seeds to a smooth paste using a suitable blender or food processor. Set aside. Heat the oil in a suitable pan or kadai over medium heat. Add the cumin seeds, mustard seeds, dry red chilies, bay leaf, cinnamon stick, cardamom pods, and cloves. Let them splutter and release their aroma. Add the peeled and slit pointed gourds (potol) to the pan and sauté for 3-4 minutes until they turn slightly golden. Add the diced potatoes to the pan and sauté for another 2-3 minutes. Add the ginger paste, garlic paste, turmeric powder, red chili powder, and salt to taste. Mix. Add the poppy seed paste to the pan and cook for 2-3 minutes. Add ½ cup of water to the pan, cover and cook on low heat for 10-12 minutes until the vegetables are cooked through and the flavors are well melded. Add slit green chilies and sugar to taste. Mix. Continue cooking for 2-3 minutes, with occasional stirring. Garnish with chopped coriander leaves. Serve hot with steamed rice or roti (Indian flatbread).Enjoy your delicious Aloo Potol Posto, a traditional Bengali stew with poppy seed paste!

# Bhuna Gour Mangsho

**Preparation time:** 15 minutes
**Cook time:** 35 minutes
**Nutrition facts (per serving):** 321 Cal (10g fat, 6.5g protein, 10g fiber)

Bhuna Gour Mangsho is a spicy and flavorful Bengali beef curry dish made by slow-cooking tender beef pieces with a mix of aromatic spices like coriander, cumin, and garam masala, along with onions, tomatoes, and ginger-garlic paste.

**Ingredients (4 servings)**
1 lb. beef, cut into chunks
½ cup plain yogurt
2 onions, finely chopped
2 tomatoes, chopped
2 tablespoons vegetable oil
1 teaspoon ginger paste
1 teaspoon garlic paste
1 teaspoon turmeric powder
1 teaspoon red chili powder
1 teaspoon cumin powder
1 teaspoon coriander powder
½ teaspoon garam masala
½ teaspoon black pepper powder
½ teaspoon sugar
Salt, to taste
Fresh coriander leaves, for garnish

### *Spice Paste*
1 cinnamon stick
5 green cardamom pods
5 cloves
1 teaspoon black peppercorns
1 teaspoon cumin seeds
1 teaspoon fennel seeds
3 dried red chilies (optional)

## Preparation

Dry roast the spices for the spice paste - cinnamon, cardamom, cloves, black peppercorns, cumin seeds, fennel seeds, and dried red chilies (if using) - in a suitable pan over low heat until fragrant. Let them cool and then grind them into a powder.

In a suitable bowl, marinate the beef chunks with yogurt, ginger paste, garlic paste, turmeric powder, red chili powder, cumin powder, coriander powder, and half of the spice paste. Mix then leave it to sit for at least 30 minutes, or refrigerate for a few hours for better flavor penetration. Heat the vegetable oil in a heavy-bottomed pan or kadai over medium heat. Toss in the finely chopped onions and sauté until golden. Add the chopped tomatoes to the pan and cook until soft and mushy. Stir in the marinated beef to the pan and cook on medium-high heat until the meat is seared and browned on all sides.

Reduce its heat to low and cover the pan. Let the beef cook slowly, with occasional stirring, until it becomes tender and releases its own juices. Once the beef is cooked, uncover the pan and cook on medium-high heat to allow any excess moisture to evaporate and the curry to thicken. Add the remaining spice paste, garam masala, black pepper powder, sugar, and salt to taste. Stir well to combine all the flavors. Cook the beef curry for a few more minutes until the spices are well-blended and the curry reaches the desired consistency. Garnish with coriander leaves and serve hot.

# Niramish Gorur Mangsho

**Preparation time:** 15 minutes
**Cook time:** 35 minutes
**Nutrition facts (per serving):** 478 Cal (11g fat, 55g protein, 3g fiber)

Niramish Gorur Mangsho is a traditional Bengali vegetarian dish made with soy chunks or potato cubes cooked in a blend of aromatic spices such as cumin, coriander, and garam masala, along with onions, tomatoes, and ginger-garlic paste.

**Ingredients (4 servings)**
1 lb. beef, cut into chunks
½ cup plain yogurt
2 tomatoes, chopped
2 tablespoons vegetable oil
1 teaspoon ginger paste
1 teaspoon turmeric powder
1 teaspoon red chili powder
1 teaspoon cumin powder
1 teaspoon coriander powder
½ teaspoon garam masala
½ teaspoon black pepper powder
½ teaspoon sugar
Salt, to taste
Fresh coriander leaves, for garnish

*Spice Paste*
1 cinnamon stick
5 green cardamom pods
5 cloves

1 teaspoon black peppercorns

1 teaspoon cumin seeds

1 teaspoon fennel seeds

3 dried red chilies (optional)

**Preparation**

Dry roast the spices for the spice paste - cinnamon, cardamom, cloves, black peppercorns, cumin seeds, fennel seeds, and dried red chilies (if using) - in a suitable pan over low heat until fragrant. Let them cool and then grind them into a powder.

In a suitable bowl, marinate the beef chunks with yogurt, ginger paste, turmeric powder, red chili powder, cumin powder, coriander powder, and half of the spice paste. Mix and leave it to sit for almost 30 minutes, or refrigerate for a few hours for better flavor penetration. Heat the vegetable oil in a heavy-bottomed pan or kadai over medium heat. Add the chopped tomatoes to the pan and cook until soft and mushy. Stir in the marinated beef to the pan and cook on medium-high heat until the meat is seared and browned on all sides.

Reduce its heat to low and cover the pan. Let the beef cook slowly, with occasional stirring, until it becomes tender and releases its own juices. Once the beef is cooked, uncover the pan and cook on medium-high heat to allow any excess moisture to evaporate and the curry to thicken. Add the remaining spice paste, garam masala, black pepper powder, sugar, and salt to taste. Stir well to combine all the flavors. Cook the beef curry for a few more minutes until the spices are well-blended and the curry reaches the desired consistency. Garnish with coriander leaves and serve hot.

# Shorshe Gorur Mangsho

**Preparation time:** 15 minutes
**Cook time:** 35 minutes
**Nutrition facts (per serving):** 391 Cal (27g fat, 27g protein, 2g fiber)

Sorshe Gorur Mangsho, also known as Bengali-style beef curry with mustard sauce, is a popular and flavorful dish in Bengal, India. It's known for its tangy and spicy flavors.

**Ingredients (4 servings)**
1 lb. beef, cut into chunks
3 tablespoons mustard seeds
3 tablespoons mustard oil
1 tablespoon turmeric powder
1 tablespoon red chili powder
1 tablespoon ginger paste
1 tablespoon garlic paste
1 tablespoon mustard paste
1 tablespoon yogurt
1 tablespoon sugar
3 green chilies, slit lengthwise
½ teaspoon nigella seeds (kalonji)
Salt, to taste
Fresh coriander leaves, for garnish

**Preparation**
In a suitable bowl, marinate the beef chunks with turmeric powder, red chili powder, ginger paste, garlic paste, mustard paste, yogurt, and salt.

Mix and leave it to sit for at least 30 minutes. Heat mustard oil in a suitable pan or kadai over medium heat. Add the mustard seeds to the hot oil and fry for a minute until they crackle and release their aroma. Be careful not to burn the mustard seeds. Remove this pan from heat and let the mustard seeds cool down. Once the mustard seeds are cool, grind them into a smooth paste using a spice grinder or mortar and pestle. You can also add a little water if needed to make a smooth paste. Heat 1 tablespoon of mustard oil in the same pan or kadai over medium heat. Add the nigella seeds (kalonji) to the hot oil and let them splutter. Add the marinated beef to the pan and cook on medium-high heat until the meat is seared and browned on all sides. Add the green chilies and sugar to the pan and Mix. Add the mustard paste to the pan and cook for a few minutes, stirring constantly. Pour in about 1 cup of water to the pan, cover it with a lid, and cook the beef on a simmer on low heat until cooked and tender. This may take around 30-40 minutes, depending on the type of beef and the size of the chunks. Once the beef is cooked, adjust the seasoning with salt and Mix. Garnish with coriander leaves and serve.

# Gorur Rezala Curry

**Preparation time:** 15 minutes
**Cook time:** 35 minutes
**Nutrition facts (per serving):** 296 Cal (7g fat, 17g protein, 4g fiber)

Gorur Rezala is a creamy and aromatic Bengali beef curry made with tender beef pieces slow-cooked in a rich gravy of yogurt, cashew paste, and a blend of aromatic spices like cinnamon, cardamom, and cloves.

## Ingredients (4 servings)
1 lb. beef, cut into chunks
1 cup yogurt
½ cup milk
½ cup heavy cream
2 tablespoons ghee or clarified butter
2 tablespoons vegetable oil
2 large onions, thinly sliced
2 tablespoons ginger paste
2 tablespoons garlic paste
1 tablespoon cashew nuts, soaked in warm water
1 tablespoon poppy seeds, soaked in warm water
3 green chilies, slit lengthwise
1 teaspoon sugar
1 teaspoon white pepper powder
½ teaspoon turmeric powder
½ teaspoon red chili powder
½ teaspoon garam masala powder
½ teaspoon cardamom powder

½ teaspoon cinnamon powder

½ teaspoon nutmeg powder

½ teaspoon mace powder

Salt, to taste

Fresh coriander leaves, for garnish

**Preparation**

In a suitable bowl, marinate the beef chunks with yogurt, ginger paste, garlic paste, and salt. Mix and leave it to sit for at least 30 minutes. In a suitable blender, make a smooth paste by grinding the soaked cashew nuts and poppy seeds with a little water. Heat ghee and oil in a suitable pan or kadai over medium heat. Stir in the thinly sliced onions to the hot oil and fry until golden in color. Toss in the marinated beef to the pan and cook on medium-high heat until the meat is seared and browned on all sides. Add the green chilies, sugar, turmeric powder, red chili powder, white pepper powder, garam masala powder, cardamom powder, cinnamon powder, nutmeg powder, and mace powder to the pan. Mix and cook for a few minutes. Add the cashew-poppy seed paste to the pan and Continue cooking for few minutes. Add milk and heavy cream to the pan and cook it to a boil. Reduce its heat to low and cook the curry on a simmer for about 30-40 minutes, or until the beef is cooked and tender. Adjust the seasoning with salt as needed. Garnish with coriander leaves and serve hot.

# Bhuri Bandhakopir Ghugni

**Preparation time:** 15 minutes
**Cook time:** 35 minutes
**Nutrition facts (per serving):** 308 Cal (10g fat, 44g protein, 0.4g fiber)

Bhuri Bandhakopir Ghugni is a traditional Bengali dish that combines beef and cabbage in a flavorful stew-like preparation. It's a comforting dish that's typically served with rice or flatbreads.

**Ingredients (4 servings)**
1 lb. beef, cut into small pieces
2 cups cabbage, shredded
½ cup yellow peas (ghugni), dried
2 medium onions, finely chopped
2 tomatoes, finely chopped
2 teaspoons ginger paste
2 teaspoons garlic paste
1 teaspoon cumin seeds
½ teaspoon turmeric powder
½ teaspoon red chili powder
½ teaspoon cumin powder
½ teaspoon coriander powder
½ teaspoon garam masala powder
¼ teaspoon cinnamon powder
2-3 green chilies, slit lengthwise
2 tablespoons oil
Salt, to taste
Fresh coriander leaves, for garnish

**Preparation**

Rinse the dried yellow peas (ghugni) thoroughly and soak them in water overnight or for at least 4-5 hours. Drain the water before using. Heat the oil in a suitable pan or kadai over medium heat. Stir in cumin seeds and let them splutter. Toss in the chopped onions and sauté until golden in color. Add the ginger paste, garlic paste, turmeric powder, red chili powder, cumin powder, coriander powder, and cinnamon powder to the pan. Mix and continue cooking it for a few minutes. Add the beef pieces to the pan and cook on medium-high heat until the meat is seared and browned on all sides. Add the soaked and drained yellow peas (ghugni) to the pan and Mix. Add the chopped tomatoes and green chilies to the pan. Cook until the tomatoes are soft. Add the shredded cabbage to the pan and Mix. Add salt to taste and enough water to cover the ingredients in the pan. Cover this pan with a lid and let the stew simmer on low heat for about 30-40 minutes, or until the beef is cooked and tender, and the flavors have melded together. Sprinkle garam masala powder over the stew and Mix. Garnish with coriander leaves and serve hot.

# Bengali Vegetable Pulao

**Preparation time:** 15 minutes

**Cook time:** 35 minutes

**Nutrition facts (per serving):** 324 Cal (16g fat, 13g protein, 3g fiber)

Bengali Vegetable Pulao is a fragrant and flavorful rice dish made with a blend of aromatic spices like cinnamon, cardamom, and cloves, cooked with a variety of fresh vegetables like carrots, peas, and potatoes, along with fried onions, raisins, and cashews.

**Ingredients (4 servings)**

2 cups Basmati rice

2 tablespoons vegetable oil

1 tablespoon ghee

1 teaspoon cumin seeds

5 green cardamom pods

5 cloves

1 cinnamon stick

1 bay leaf

1 onion, thinly sliced

2 carrots, diced

1 cup peas

1 cup cauliflower florets, diced

1 cup green beans, chopped

1 tablespoon ginger paste

1 tablespoon garlic paste

1 teaspoon turmeric powder

1 teaspoon red chili powder

Salt, to taste

4 cups water

2 tablespoons chopped cilantro (coriander) leaves

**Preparation**

Drain and set aside. Heat the oil and ghee in a suitable heavy-bottomed pot over medium heat. Add the cumin seeds, cardamom pods, cloves, cinnamon stick, and bay leaf. Sauté for a few seconds until the spices are fragrant. Toss in the sliced onions and sauté until they turn translucent. Add the diced carrots, peas, cauliflower florets, and green beans. Sauté for 5-6 minutes. Add the ginger paste, garlic paste, turmeric powder, red chili powder, and salt. Mix and sauté for a few more minutes. Stir in the drained rice and sauté for a few minutes until the rice is well coated with the spices. Add 4 cups of water and cook to a boil. Reduce its heat to low and cover the pot. Cook for on a simmer 20 minutes. Remove from heat and leave for 5 minutes. Serve.

# Bengali Shorshe Bhaat

**Preparation time:** 15 minutes
**Cook time:** 35 minutes
**Nutrition facts (per serving):** 557 Cal (19g fat, 33g protein, 5g fiber)

Bengali Shorshe Bhaat is a traditional rice dish from West Bengal that is flavored with mustard seeds and green chilies. Cooked with mustard oil, this simple and easy-to-make dish is a popular everyday meal in Bengali households.

## Ingredients (4 servings)
1 cup Basmati rice
1 tablespoon black mustard seeds
2 green chili peppers, slit lengthwise
1 tablespoon vegetable oil
1 tablespoon mustard oil
½ teaspoon turmeric powder
Salt, to taste
Water, as needed

## Preparation
Drain and set aside. In a suitable blender or a mortar and pestle, grind the black mustard seeds to a fine powder. In a suitable bowl, combine the rice, mustard powder, slit green chili peppers, vegetable oil, mustard oil, turmeric powder, and salt. Mix. Add enough water to the rice mixture to cover it by about 1 inch. Stir well. Transfer the rice mixture to a pressure cooker or a suitable pot. If using a pot, cover it with a lid. If using a pressure cooker, cook the rice on high heat for 2 whistles. If using a pot,

cook on low heat for 20 minutes. Once your rice is cooked, remove from heat and leave for 5 minutes. Serve.

# Bengali Ghee Bhaat

**Preparation time:** 15 minutes

**Cook time:** 35 minutes

**Nutrition facts (per serving):** 308 Cal (10g fat, 44g protein, 0.4g fiber)

Bengali Ghee Bhaat is a fragrant and rich rice dish made with clarified butter or ghee and cumin seeds, which introduces a unique flavor and aroma. This traditional dish is often served during special occasions, celebrations, and festivals.

## Ingredients (4 servings)

1 cup Basmati rice

2 tablespoons ghee (clarified butter)

2 green cardamom pods

2 cloves

1 cinnamon stick

1 bay leaf

2 cups water

Salt, to taste

## Preparation

Drain and set aside. In a suitable pot or a pressure cooker, heat the ghee over medium heat. Add the green cardamom pods, cloves, cinnamon stick, and bay leaf. Sauté for a few seconds until the spices are fragrant. Stir in the drained rice to the pot and sauté for a few minutes. Stir in 2 cups of water and salt to taste. Mix. If using a pressure cooker, cook the rice on high heat for 2 whistles. If using a pot, cover it with a lid and cook it on a low heat for 20 minutes. Once your rice is cooked, remove from heat and leave for 5 minutes. Fluff the rice with a fork and transfer to a serving bowl. Your Bengali Ghee Bhaat is ready to be served!

# Bengali Basanti Pulao

**Preparation time:** 15 minutes
**Cook time:** 35 minutes
**Nutrition facts (per serving):** 292 Cal (13g fat, 41g protein, 0.5g fiber)

Bengali Basanti Pulao is a sweet and aromatic rice dish that's flavored with saffron and infused with raisins, cashews, and bay leaves. It's a popular dish in Bengali cuisine and is often enjoyed during special occasions and festivals.

## Ingredients (4 servings)

1 cup Basmati rice
2 tablespoons ghee (clarified butter)
2 tablespoons sugar
¼ teaspoon saffron threads
2 green cardamom pods
2 cloves
1 cinnamon stick
1 bay leaf
2 cups water
Salt, to taste
2 tablespoons golden raisins
2 tablespoons cashew nuts
2 tablespoons almonds, sliced

## Preparation

Drain and set aside. In a suitable pot or a pressure cooker, heat the ghee over medium heat. Add the green cardamom pods, cloves, cinnamon stick, and bay leaf. Sauté for a few seconds until the spices are fragrant. Stir in the drained rice to the pot and sauté for 2-3 minutes until the rice is well coated with the ghee. Pour in about 2 cups of water and salt to taste. Mix. In a suitable bowl, soak the saffron threads in 2 tablespoons of warm milk. Add the sugar and soaked saffron to the pot. Mix. If using a pressure cooker, cook the rice on high heat for 2 whistles. If using a pot, cover it with a lid and cook on low heat for 20 minutes. Once your rice is cooked, remove from heat and leave for 5 minutes. In a suitable pan, roast the raisins, cashew nuts, and sliced almonds until lightly browned. Fluff the rice with a fork and transfer to a serving bowl. Garnish the Basanti Pulao with the roasted raisins, cashew nuts, and sliced almonds. Your Bengali Basanti Pulao is ready to be served!

# Bengali Mishti Pulao

**Preparation time:** 15 minutes
**Cook time:** 35 minutes
**Nutrition facts (per serving):** 432 Cal (14g fat, 30g protein, 1.3g fiber)

Bengali Mishti Pulao is a sweet and fragrant rice dish made with a mix of spices, raisins, cashews, and sugar. It's a popular dish in Bengali cuisine and is often served during special occasions, celebrations, and festivals.

## Ingredients (4 servings)
1 cup Basmati rice
2 tablespoons ghee (clarified butter)
½ cup sugar
¼ cup milk
2 green cardamom pods
2 cloves
1 cinnamon stick
1 bay leaf
2 cups water
Salt, to taste
2 tablespoons cashew nuts
2 tablespoons raisins
1 tablespoon sliced almonds
A few strands of saffron (optional)

## Preparation
Drain and set aside. In a suitable pot or a pressure cooker, heat the ghee over medium heat. Add the green cardamom pods, cloves, cinnamon

stick, and bay leaf. Sauté for a few seconds until the spices are fragrant. Stir in the drained rice to the pot and sauté for 2 minutes until the rice is well coated with the ghee. Pour in about 2 cups of water and salt to taste. Mix. If using a pressure cooker, cook the rice on high heat for 2 whistles. If using a pot, cover it with a lid and cook on low heat for 20 minutes. In a separate pan, heat the milk and sugar together until the sugar dissolves. Keep stirring until the milk thickens slightly. Once your rice is cooked, remove from heat and leave for 5 minutes. Add the milk-sugar mixture to the rice and Mix. If desired, add a few strands of saffron for flavor and color. In a suitable pan, roast the cashew nuts, raisins, and sliced almonds until lightly browned. Fluff the rice with a fork and transfer to a serving bowl. Garnish the Mishti Pulao with the roasted cashew nuts, raisins, and sliced almonds. Your Bengali Mishti Pulao is ready to be served!

# Bengali Lemon Rice

**Preparation time:** 15 minutes

**Cook time:** 35 minutes

**Nutrition facts (per serving):** 259 Cal (5 g fat, 23g protein, 6g fiber)

Bengali Lemon Rice is a simple and tangy rice dish that is flavored with lemon juice, mustard seeds, and curry leaves. Here's a popular dish in Bengali cuisine and is often enjoyed with fish or chicken curry.

## Ingredients (4 servings)

1 cup Basmati rice, rinsed and soaked

2 tablespoons oil

1 teaspoon mustard seeds

1 teaspoon cumin seeds

¼ teaspoon asafetida (Hing)

2-3 green chilies, slit

¼ teaspoon turmeric powder

Salt, to taste

2 tablespoons lemon juice

2 tablespoons chopped coriander leaves (cilantro)

## Preparation

Drain and set aside. In a suitable pot or a pressure cooker, heat the oil over medium heat. Add the mustard seeds and cumin seeds. When the seeds start to splutter, add the asafetida and green chilies. Sauté for a few seconds until the spices are fragrant. Stir in the drained rice to the pot and sauté for 2 minutes until the rice is well coated with the spices. Pour in almost 2 cups of water and salt to taste. Mix. If using a pressure cooker, cook the rice on high heat for 2 whistles. If using a pot, cover it with a lid and cook on low heat for 20 minutes. Once your rice is cooked, remove from heat and leave for 5 minutes. Add the lemon juice and the turmeric powder to the rice and Mix. Garnish with chopped coriander leaves. Your Bengali Lemon Rice is ready to be served!

# Bengali Tomato Rice

**Preparation time:** 15 minutes
**Cook time:** 35 minutes
**Nutrition facts (per serving):** 382 Cal (13g fat, 9g protein, 6g fiber)

Bengali Tomato Rice, also known as "Tomato Pulao" is a flavorful rice dish made with ripe tomatoes, spices, and vegetables. It's a popular dish in Bengali cuisine and is often served as an entrée with a side of raita or salad. The dish has a tangy and slightly spicy taste and is a perfect choice for a wholesome meal.

## Ingredients (4 servings)

1 cup Basmati rice
2 tablespoons oil
1 teaspoon cumin seeds
1 onion, finely chopped
3 tomatoes, finely chopped
1 green chili, slit
¼ teaspoon turmeric powder
Salt, to taste
½ teaspoon garam masala powder
2 tablespoons chopped coriander leaves (cilantro)

## Preparation

Drain and set aside. In a suitable pot or a pressure cooker, heat the oil over medium heat. Add the cumin seeds. When the seeds start to splutter, add the chopped onion and green chili. Sauté until the onion turns translucent. Add the chopped tomatoes to the pot and sauté for 2 minutes until the tomatoes are soft and mushy. Add the turmeric powder and salt to taste. Mix. Stir in the drained rice to the pot and sauté for 2 minutes until the rice is well coated with the tomato-onion mixture. Pour in about 2 cups of water and Mix. If using a pressure cooker, cook the rice on high heat for 2 whistles. If using a pot, cover it with a lid and cook on low heat for 20 minutes. Once your rice is cooked, remove from heat and leave for 5 minutes. Add garam masala powder and chopped coriander leaves to the rice and Mix. Your Bengali Tomato Rice is ready to be served!

# Bengali Narkel Bhaat

**Preparation time:** 15 minutes
**Cook time:** 35 minutes
**Nutrition facts (per serving):** 212 Cal (9g fat, 7g protein, 0.5g fiber)

Bengali Narkel Bhaat, also known as "Coconut Rice" is a fragrant rice dish that is flavored with grated coconut, spices, and ghee. It's a popular dish in Bengali cuisine and is served with fish or vegetable curry. The dish has a rich and nutty taste and is a perfect choice for a special occasion or a holiday festival.

## Ingredients (4 servings)

1 cup Basmati rice, soaked and rinsed
1 tablespoon ghee or oil
½ teaspoon cumin seeds
1 bay leaf
1 cinnamon stick
3 green cardamoms, crushed
2 cloves
¼ teaspoon turmeric powder
Salt, to taste
1 cup coconut milk
½ cup water
2 tablespoons grated coconut
2 tablespoons chopped coriander leaves (cilantro)

**Preparation**

In a suitable pot or pressure cooker, heat up some ghee or oil over medium heat. Stir in the cumin seeds, bay leaf, cinnamon stick, green cardamoms, and cloves, and sauté until the spices are fragrant. Stir in the drained rice to the pot and sauté for a few minutes, ensuring that the rice is coated with the spices. Season with turmeric powder and salt, mixing well. Pour in the coconut milk and water, mixing thoroughly. If using a pressure cooker, cook the rice on high heat for two whistles. Otherwise, cover the pot with a lid and cook on low heat for 20 minutes. Add grated coconut and chopped coriander leaves to the rice and Mix. Your Bengali Narkel Bhaat (Coconut Rice) is ready to be served!

# Vegetable biryani

**Preparation time:** 15 minutes

**Cook time:** 35 minutes

**Nutrition facts (per serving):** 270 Cal (12g fat, 4g protein,6 g fiber)

Vegetable biryani is a classic Indian rice dish made with fragrant basmati rice, mixed vegetables, and a blend of aromatic spices. It's a popular vegetarian option to enjoy.

## Ingredients (4 servings)

### *Rice*

2 cups basmati rice, rinsed and soaked

5 cups water

1 bay leaf

4 green cardamoms

4 cloves

1 cinnamon stick

Salt, to taste

### *Vegetables*

2 tablespoons oil

1 onion, sliced

3 green chilies, slit

1 tablespoon ginger-garlic paste

2 cups mixed vegetables (carrots, peas, potatoes, beans, cauliflower)

1 teaspoon red chili powder

1 teaspoon coriander powder

½ teaspoon cumin powder

½ teaspoon garam masala powder

Salt, to taste

½ cup yogurt

### *Assembling*
Fried onions, for garnish

Chopped coriander leaves (cilantro), for garnish

Saffron, soaked in milk

### Preparation
In a suitable pot, cook the water to a boil. Add the bay leaf, green cardamoms, cloves, cinnamon stick, and salt to the water. Drain your soaked rice and add it to the pot. Cook until the rice is about 80% done. Drain and set aside. In a suitable pan, heat oil over medium heat. Add the sliced onion and green chilies and sauté until the onions are golden in color. Stir in the ginger-garlic paste and sauté for another minute.

Add the mixed vegetables and sauté for a few minutes until the vegetables are partially cooked. Add the garam masala powder, red chili powder, coriander and cumin powder, and salt to the pan. Mix. Add the yogurt to the pan and Mix. Continue cooking for 2-3 minutes until the vegetables are fully cooked. Preheat the oven to 350°F.

Grease a suitable baking dish with oil. Add a layer of rice to the bottom of the dish. Add a layer of the vegetable mixture on top of the rice. Repeat these layers until all the rice and vegetables have been used up. Top the final layer of rice with saffron milk and fried onions. Cover this dish with a lid or foil and bake this dish in the preheated oven for 20-25 minutes. Garnish with coriander leaves and serve.

# Aloo paratha

**Preparation time:** 15 minutes

**Cook time:** 35 minutes

**Nutrition facts (per serving):** 232 Cal (14g fat, 7g protein, 1.3g fiber)

Aloo paratha is a popular Indian flatbread stuffed with a spiced potato filling. It's usually served with yogurt, chutney, or pickle and can be enjoyed as a main dish or a breakfast item.

## Ingredients (4 servings)

2 cups whole wheat flour

½ teaspoon salt

Water, as needed

2-3 medium-sized potatoes, boiled and mashed

1 teaspoon cumin seeds

1 teaspoon coriander powder

½ teaspoon red chili powder

¼ teaspoon turmeric powder

Salt, to taste

Oil or ghee, as needed for cooking

## Preparation

In a suitable mixing bowl, combine the whole wheat flour and salt. Slowly pour in water as needed and knead into a soft dough. Cover and set aside for 10-15 minutes. In a separate suitable mixing bowl, combine the mashed potatoes, cumin seeds, coriander powder, red chili powder, turmeric powder, and salt. Mix. Divide the prepared dough into equal-sized balls. Take 1 ball and roll it out into a suitable circle on a floured surface. Place a spoonful of the potato mixture in the center of the circle. Bring the edges of the circle together and pinch to seal the potato mixture inside. Roll out the stuffed ball into a flat disc, dusting with flour as needed to prevent sticking. Heat a tawa or griddle over medium-high heat. Place the rolled-out paratha on the hot tawa or griddle and cook for 1-2 minutes until bubbles start to appear. Flip the paratha and brush it with oil or ghee. Cook the paratha for another 1-2 minutes until both sides are golden in color and crispy. Repeat with its remaining dough and potato mixture. Your aloo parathas are ready to be served!

# Aloo Qeema

**Preparation time:** 15 minutes
**Cook time:** 35 minutes
**Nutrition facts (per serving):** 268 Cal (26g fat, 9g protein, 0.3g fiber)

Aloo Qeema is a Pakistani and North Indian dish made with ground beef and potatoes cooked in a flavorful blend of spices such as cumin, coriander, and garam masala. It's often served with rice, naan bread, or roti.

**Ingredients (4 servings)**
1 lb. ground beef or lamb
2 tablespoons oil
1 onion, finely chopped
3 garlic cloves, minced
1 tablespoon ginger paste
1 teaspoon cumin seeds
1 teaspoon coriander powder
½ teaspoon turmeric powder
½ teaspoon red chili powder
Salt, to taste
4 potatoes, peeled and cubed
½ cup water
Fresh coriander leaves, for garnish

**Preparation**
Heat the oil in a suitable pot over medium-high heat. Stir in the cumin seeds and let them splutter for a few seconds. Add the chopped onions

and sauté until golden. Add the minced garlic and ginger paste and sauté for another minute. Add the ground beef or lamb to the pot and cook until browned. Stir in the coriander powder, turmeric powder, red chili powder, and salt to the pot. Mix. Add the cubed potatoes to the pot and Mix. Pour in ½ cup of water and Mix. Cover the pot and Cook it on a simmer over low heat for 20 minutes. Garnish with chopped fresh coriander leaves and serve hot with naan, roti, or rice.

# Mixed Sabzi

**Preparation time:** 15 minutes
**Cook time:** 35 minutes
**Nutrition facts (per serving):** 249 Cal (7g fat, 2g protein, 3g fiber)

Mixed sabzi is a vegetarian dish from the Indian subcontinent made with a variety of vegetables such as potatoes, carrots, peas, and cauliflower, cooked in a blend of spices and herbs.

## Ingredients (4 servings)

2 tablespoons oil
1 onion, finely chopped
3 garlic cloves, minced
1 tablespoon ginger paste
1 teaspoon cumin seeds
1 teaspoon coriander powder
½ teaspoon turmeric powder
½ teaspoon red chili powder (adjust to taste)
Salt, to taste
3 potatoes, peeled and cubed
3 carrots, peeled and sliced
2 bell peppers, sliced
1 cup green beans, trimmed and chopped
1 cup peas
2 tomatoes, chopped
Water, as needed
Fresh coriander leaves, for garnish

**Preparation**

Heat the oil in a suitable pot over medium-high heat. Stir in the cumin seeds and let them splutter for a few seconds. Add the chopped onions and sauté until golden. Add the minced garlic and the ginger paste and sauté for another minute. Stir in the coriander powder, turmeric powder, red chili powder, and salt to the pot. Mix. Add the cubed potatoes, sliced carrots, and chopped tomatoes to the pot. Mix. Add the sliced bell peppers, green beans, and peas to the pot. Mix. Pour in enough water to cover the vegetables. Cover the pot and Cook it on a simmer over low heat for 20 minutes. Garnish with chopped fresh coriander leaves and serve hot with naan, roti, or rice. Your mixed sabzi is now ready to be served! It's a nutritious and flavorful dish that's perfect for a vegetarian meal or as a side dish with your favorite main course.

# Saag

**Preparation time:** 15 minutes
**Cook time:** 35 minutes
**Nutrition facts (per serving):** 211 Cal (1.2g fat, 8g protein, 7g fiber)

Saag is a popular North Indian dish made with leafy greens such as spinach, mustard greens or fenugreek leaves. It's usually served with roti, naan or rice.

## Ingredients (4 servings)
1 bunch spinach leaves, washed and chopped
1 bunch mustard greens or kale, washed and chopped
1 onion, chopped
3 garlic cloves, minced
1 tablespoon ginger paste
3 green chilies, chopped (optional)
2 tablespoons oil or ghee
1 teaspoon cumin seeds
1 teaspoon coriander powder
½ teaspoon turmeric powder
½ teaspoon red chili powder (adjust to taste)
Salt, to taste
½ cup water
¼ cup heavy cream (optional)
Fresh coriander leaves, for garnish

**Preparation**

Heat the oil or ghee in a suitable pot over medium-high heat. Stir in the cumin seeds and let them splutter for a few seconds. Add the chopped onions and sauté until golden. Add the minced garlic, ginger paste, and green chilies (if using) and sauté for another minute. Stir in the coriander powder, turmeric powder, red chili powder, and salt to the pot. Mix. Add the chopped spinach and mustard greens or kale to the pot. Mix. Pour in ½ cup of water and Mix. Cover the pot and Cook it on a simmer over low heat for 20 minutes. Remove this pot from heat and let it cool slightly. Use an immersion blender or transfer the prepared mixture to a suitable blender and blend until smooth. Return the pot to the stove and heat over low heat. Add the heavy cream (if using) and mix. Garnish with chopped fresh coriander leaves and serve hot with naan, roti, or rice. Your saag is now ready to be served! It's a delicious and healthy dish that's perfect for a vegetarian meal or as a side dish with your favorite main course.

# Masala Gobhi

**Preparation time:** 15 minutes
**Cook time:** 35 minutes
**Nutrition facts (per serving):** 367 Cal (21g fat, 9g protein, 1.2g fiber)

Masala Gobhi is a popular dish made with cauliflower florets cooked with a blend of aromatic spices and herbs, resulting in a delicious and flavorful vegetarian dish that can be enjoyed as a side or main course. It's a perfect combination of spice and crunch.

### Ingredients (4 servings)
1 head cauliflower, cut into florets
1 onion, chopped
3 garlic cloves, minced
1 tablespoon ginger paste
3 green chilies, chopped (optional)
2 tablespoons oil
1 teaspoon cumin seeds
1 teaspoon coriander powder
½ teaspoon turmeric powder
½ teaspoon red chili powder (adjust to taste)
Salt, to taste
2 tomatoes, chopped
½ cup water
Chopped fresh coriander (cilantro) leaves, for garnish

**Preparation**

Heat the oil in a suitable pan over medium-high heat. Stir in the cumin seeds and let them splutter for a few seconds. Add chopped onions and sauté until golden. Add the minced garlic, ginger paste, and green chilies (if using) and sauté for another minute. Stir in the coriander powder, turmeric powder, red chili powder, and salt to the pan. Mix. Add cauliflower florets to the pan and Mix. Add the chopped tomatoes and ½ cup of water to the pan. Mix. Cover the pan and Cook it over low heat for 20 minutes until the cauliflower is cooked and tender. Garnish with chopped fresh coriander leaves and serve hot with naan, roti, or rice. Your masala gobi is now ready to be served! It's a delicious and healthy vegetarian dish that's perfect for a weekday dinner or a special occasion.

# Bengali Stuffed Eggplant (Begun Bhaja)

**Preparation time:** 15 minutes
**Cook time:** 35 minutes
**Nutrition facts (per serving):** 265 Cal (5g fat, 7g protein, 5g fiber)

Bengali stuffed eggplant, also known as "Begun Bhaja," is a popular vegetarian dish made by stuffing eggplants with a mixture of spices and frying them until crispy on the outside and soft on the inside.

## Ingredients (4 servings)
4 small eggplants (about 3 inches long)
1 onion, finely chopped
3 garlic cloves, minced
1 tablespoon ginger paste
2 green chilies, finely chopped
2 tablespoons oil
1 teaspoon cumin seeds
1 teaspoon coriander powder
½ teaspoon turmeric powder
½ teaspoon red chili powder
Salt, to taste
2 tablespoons chopped fresh coriander leaves

## Stuffing
1 potato, boiled and mashed
½ cup green peas
½ cup chopped carrots

¼ cup chopped cauliflower

¼ cup chopped green beans

1 teaspoon cumin seeds

1 teaspoon coriander powder

½ teaspoon turmeric powder

½ teaspoon red chili powder (adjust to taste)

Salt, to taste

2 tablespoons oil

## Preparation

Wash and pat dry the eggplants. Make 4 slits in each eggplant, taking care not to cut all the way through. Heat the oil in a suitable pan over medium heat. Stir in cumin seeds and let them splutter for a few seconds. Add the onions, garlic, ginger, and green chilies and sauté until the onions are golden in color. Stir in the coriander powder, turmeric powder, red chili powder, and salt to the pan. Mix. Add the mashed potato, green peas, carrots, cauliflower, and green beans to the pan. Mix. Cover this pan and cook over low heat for 10-12 minutes until the vegetables are cooked and tender. Remove this pan from heat and let it cool slightly. Stuff the eggplants with the vegetable mixture using a spoon or your fingers. Heat oil in a suitable pan over medium heat. Add the stuffed eggplants to the pan and cook for almost 7 minutes per side, until golden in color and tender. Garnish with chopped fresh coriander leaves and serve hot with steamed rice or roti. Your Bengali-style stuffed eggplant is now ready to be served! It's a flavorful and delicious dish that's perfect for a special occasion or a festive meal.

# Bengali Style Stir-Fried Eggplant

**Preparation time:** 15 minutes
**Cook time:** 35 minutes
**Nutrition facts (per serving):** 221 Cal (11g fat, 4g protein, 1.4g fiber)

Bengali style stir-fried eggplant is a popular and simple Bengali side dish made by pan-frying slices of eggplant until tender and crispy with a sprinkle of spices.

## Ingredients (4 servings)
2 medium-sized eggplants
1 teaspoon turmeric powder
Salt, to taste
1 teaspoon red chili powder
1 tablespoon mustard oil (or any vegetable oil)
½ teaspoon nigella seeds (kalonji)
½ teaspoon cumin seeds
2 green chilies, chopped
1 tablespoon grated ginger
¼ cup fresh coriander leaves

## Preparation
Wash and dry the eggplants. Cut off the stem and cut the eggplants into 1-inch cubes. In a suitable mixing bowl, add turmeric powder, salt, and red chili powder. Mix and then add the eggplant cubes. Toss the eggplant cubes in the spice mix until well coated. Heat the mustard oil in a suitable frying pan over medium heat. When the oil is hot, add the nigella seeds and cumin seeds. Fry for a few seconds until they start to splutter. Add

the chopped green chilies and grated ginger. Sauté for 2 minutes until the ginger starts to turn golden in color. Add the coated eggplant cubes to the frying pan. Mix and fry for 5-7 minutes until the eggplant cubes are soft and tender. Turn off its heat and garnish with chopped fresh coriander leaves. Your Bengali-style stir-fried eggplant is now ready to be served!

# Bengali Aloo Posto

**Preparation time:** 15 minutes
**Cook time:** 35 minutes
**Nutrition facts (per serving):** 317 Cal (17g fat, 5g protein, 0.8g fiber)

Bengali Aloo Posto is a classic dish made with potatoes and poppy seed paste, cooked with mustard oil and flavored with spices. It's a simple yet flavorful vegetarian dish often served with steamed rice.

### Ingredients (4 servings)
4 medium-sized potatoes, peeled and cut into small cubes
½ cup poppy seeds
2 green chilies, chopped
1 teaspoon mustard or any other oil
½ teaspoon nigella seeds (kalonji)
Salt, to taste

### Preparation
Soak the poppy seeds in warm water for 20 minutes. Drain the water and grind the poppy seeds to a fine paste in a suitable blender. Heat the mustard oil in a suitable frying pan over medium heat. When the oil is hot, add the nigella seeds and sauté for a few seconds until they start to splutter. Add the chopped green chilies and fry for a minute or two until they start to soften. Add the potato cubes to the frying pan and fry for 5 minutes until they start to turn golden in color. Add the poppy seed paste and mix. Add a cup of water, salt to taste, and mix. Cover the frying pan with a lid and simmer for 20 minutes. Turn off its heat and garnish with chopped fresh coriander leaves. Your Bengali-style Aloo Posto is now ready to be served!

# Bengali Chicken Rezala

**Preparation time:** 15 minutes
**Cook time:** 35 minutes
**Nutrition facts (per serving):** 202 Cal (7g fat, 6g protein, 1.3g fiber)

Bengali Chicken Rezala is a creamy and aromatic chicken curry made with yogurt, cashew nut paste, and a blend of aromatic spices. Here's a popular dish in Bengali cuisine and is typically served with steamed rice or naan bread.

## Ingredients (4 servings)

2 lbs. chicken, cut into medium-sized pieces

1 cup yogurt

1 tablespoon ginger paste

1 tablespoon garlic paste

½ teaspoon turmeric powder

1 teaspoon cumin powder

1 teaspoon coriander powder

½ teaspoon garam masala powder

½ cup cashew nut paste

½ cup onion paste

½ cup ghee or vegetable oil

2 bay leaves

2 cinnamon sticks

3 green cardamoms

3 cloves

Salt, to taste

**Preparation**

In a suitable mixing bowl, add the yogurt, ginger paste, garlic paste, turmeric powder, cumin powder, coriander powder, garam masala powder, and salt. Mix and marinate the chicken pieces in the prepared mixture for at least 2 hours. Warm up the ghee or vegetable oil in a suitable frying pan over medium heat. When the oil is hot, add bay leaves, cinnamon sticks, green cardamoms, and cloves. Fry for a few seconds until they start to release their aroma. Add the onion paste and fry for a few minutes until it turns golden in color. Add the marinated chicken pieces to the frying pan and mix. Fry for a few minutes until the chicken pieces start to turn golden in color. Add the cashew nut paste and mix. Add a cup of water, cover the frying pan with a lid, and simmer for 20-25 minutes until the chicken pieces are fully cooked and the gravy thickens. Turn off its heat and garnish with chopped fresh coriander leaves. Your Bengali-style Chicken Rezala is now ready to be served! This dish can be enjoyed as a main course with rice or naan.

# Bengali Aloo Dum

**Preparation time:** 15 minutes
**Cook time:** 35 minutes
**Nutrition facts (per serving):** 393 Cal (18g g fat, 9g protein, 3g fiber)

Bengali Aloo Dum is a popular potato curry cooked in a spicy yogurt-based gravy with a blend of aromatic spices. It's a flavorful and comforting dish often served with rice or Indian flatbreads like roti or paratha.

## Ingredients (4 servings)

5 medium-sized potatoes, peeled and cut into halves
1 onion, chopped
1 tablespoon ginger paste
1 tablespoon garlic paste
3 green chilies, chopped
½ teaspoon turmeric powder
1 teaspoon cumin powder
1 teaspoon coriander powder
½ teaspoon red chili powder
½ teaspoon garam masala powder
½ cup tomato puree
¼ cup mustard oil (or any vegetable oil)
Salt, to taste
1 tablespoon fresh coriander leaves, for garnishing

## Preparation

Boil the potato halves until half-cooked. Drain the water and keep the potatoes aside. Heat the mustard oil in a suitable frying pan over medium heat. When the oil is hot, add the chopped onions and fry until they turn golden in color. Add the ginger paste, garlic paste, and chopped green chilies. Fry for a few seconds until they release their aroma. Add the garam masala powder, cumin, turmeric, coriander, and red chili powder, and salt. Mix. Add the tomato puree and Mix. Cook for a few minutes until the tomato puree thickens. Add the potato halves to the frying pan and mix. Fry for a few minutes until the potatoes are well coated with the spice mixture. Add a cup of water, cover the frying pan with a lid, and simmer for 20 minutes until the potatoes are fully cooked and the gravy thickens. Turn off its heat and garnish with chopped fresh coriander leaves. Your Bengali-style Aloo Dum is now ready to be served!

# Bengali Masoor Dal

**Preparation time:** 15 minutes
**Cook time:** 35 minutes
**Nutrition facts (per serving):** 181 Cal (6g fat, 2.4g protein, 0.6g fiber)

Bengali Masoor Dal is a popular and comforting lentil soup made with red lentils, spices, and vegetables. It's usually served with rice and makes for a satisfying and nutritious meal.

**Ingredients (4 servings)**
1 cup Masoor Dal (red lentils), rinsed
3 cups water
1 onion, chopped
1 tablespoon ginger paste
1 tablespoon garlic paste
1 tomato, chopped
1 teaspoon turmeric powder
1 teaspoon cumin powder
½ teaspoon coriander powder
½ teaspoon red chili powder
½ teaspoon garam masala powder
3 green chilies, chopped
3 tablespoons mustard oil (or any vegetable oil)
Salt, to taste
Fresh coriander leaves, for garnishing

**Preparation**

In your pressure cooker, add the rinsed dal, water, chopped onion, ginger paste, garlic paste, chopped tomato, turmeric powder, cumin powder, coriander powder, red chili powder, garam masala powder, chopped green chilies, mustard oil, and salt. Mix all the ingredients well and cook the dal for 4-5 whistles or until fully cooked. Release the pressure then open the pressure lid and check the consistency of the dal. Add some water to adjust the consistency. Garnish this dal with coriander leaves and serve hot with steamed rice.

# Spicy Puffed Rice

**Preparation time:** 15 minutes
**Cook time:** 35 minutes
**Nutrition facts (per serving):** 101 Cal (7g fat, 1.3g protein, 1g fiber)

Kolkata Street Style Jhal Muri is a popular spicy snack made with puffed rice, peanuts, vegetables, and a tangy tamarind sauce, commonly sold by street vendors in Kolkata.

## Ingredients (4 servings)
2 cups puffed rice
1 onion, chopped
1 tomato, chopped
1 green chili, chopped
½ cup boiled potatoes, chopped
¼ cup roasted peanuts
¼ cup roasted chana dal (split chickpeas)
1 tablespoon mustard oil
½ teaspoon turmeric powder
½ teaspoon red chili powder
½ teaspoon cumin powder
½ teaspoon coriander powder
½ teaspoon chaat masala
Salt, to taste
Fresh coriander leaves, for garnishing
Lemon wedges, for serving

## Preparation

Heat the mustard oil in a suitable pan over medium heat. Add the chopped onion and green chili and fry for a few minutes until the onions are translucent. Add the chopped tomato and fry for another minute. Add the turmeric powder, red chili powder, cumin powder, coriander powder, and salt. Mix. Add the boiled potatoes and mix. Cook for a few minutes until the potatoes are well coated with the spice mixture. Add the puffed rice to the pan and mix. Add the roasted peanuts and chana dal to the pan and Mix. Add the chaat masala and mix. Turn off its heat and garnish with coriander leaves. Serve the Jhal Muri with lemon wedges. Your Kolkata street style Jhal Muri is now ready to be served! This spicy snack is perfect for tea time or as a quick bite. Enjoy!

# Bengali Aloo Sheddo

**Preparation time:** 15 minutes
**Cook time:** 35 minutes
**Nutrition facts (per serving):** 374 Cal (14g fat, 7g protein, 2g fiber)

Bengali Aloo Sheddo or Alu Sheddho is a simple, traditional mashed potato dish, typically served with a drizzle of mustard oil and a sprinkle of salt. It's a comfort food and often eaten with steamed rice and dal.

## Ingredients (4 servings)
5 medium-sized potatoes, peeled and chopped
1 tablespoon mustard oil
2 green chilies, chopped
Salt, to taste
Water, as needed
Ghee, for serving

## Preparation
In a pot, add the chopped potatoes, chopped green chilies, and enough water to cover the potatoes. Add salt to taste and mic. Cook the water to a boil and then Reduce its heat to low. Cook the potatoes on low heat until fully cooked and soft. Once the potatoes are fully cooked, remove them from the heat and drain the water. Mash the cooked potatoes with a fork until smooth and free of lumps. Add the mustard oil to the mashed potatoes and mix. Serve the Aloo Sheddo hot with a dollop of ghee on top. Your Bengali Aloo Sheddo is now ready to be served! This dish is simple yet flavorful and is a popular comfort food in Bengali cuisine. Enjoy with steamed rice and dal for a complete meal.

# Doi Murgi

**Preparation time:** 15 minutes

**Cook time:** 35 minutes

**Nutrition facts (per serving):** 331 Cal (16g fat, 4g protein, 2g fiber)

Doi Murgi is a classic Bengali dish made with chicken cooked in a yogurt-based gravy along with aromatic spices. It is a creamy and flavorful curry that's best served with steamed rice or pulao.

## Ingredients (4 servings)

1 lb. chicken, cut into pieces

½ cup plain yogurt

1 onion, chopped

1 tomato, chopped

1 tablespoon ginger paste

1 tablespoon garlic paste

3 green chilies, slit

1 teaspoon cumin powder

1 teaspoon coriander powder

½ teaspoon turmeric powder

½ teaspoon red chili powder

Salt, to taste

2 tablespoons oil

Fresh coriander leaves, for garnishing

## Preparation

Marinate the chicken with the yogurt, ginger paste, garlic paste, cumin powder, coriander powder, turmeric powder, and salt. Mix and keep it aside for at least 30 minutes. Heat the oil in a suitable pan over medium heat. Add the chopped onion and green chilies and fry until the onions are translucent. Add the chopped tomato and fry for another minute. Place the marinated chicken in the pan and mix. Cook the chicken on medium heat until fully cooked and tender. Add salt to taste and mix. Turn off its heat and garnish with coriander leaves. Serve the Doi Murgi hot with steamed rice or chapati. Your Bengali Style Yogurt Chicken Curry is now ready to be served! The yogurt gives the chicken a creamy and tangy flavor that goes perfectly with the spices. Enjoy this classic Bengali dish with your family and friends.

# Bangladeshi Style Chana Dal

**Preparation time:** 15 minutes
**Cook time:** 37 minutes
**Nutrition facts (per serving):** 249 Cal (0g fat, 1.1g protein, 0g fiber)

Bangladeshi Style Chana Dal is a popular vegetarian dish made with split Bengal gram lentils, onions, tomatoes, and spices. It's typically served with rice or flatbreads and is a staple in Bengali cuisine.

## Ingredients (4 servings)

1 cup chana dal (Bengal gram lentils)

3 cups water

1 tablespoon oil or ghee

1 onion, chopped

1 tomato, chopped

1 tablespoon ginger paste

1 tablespoon garlic paste

1 teaspoon cumin powder

1 teaspoon coriander powder

½ teaspoon turmeric powder

Salt, to taste

3 green chilies, slit

Fresh coriander leaves, for garnishing

## Preparation

Rinse the chana dal in cold water and soak it in enough water for at least 30 minutes. Drain the water from the dal and add it to a suitable pot with 2-3 cups of water. Add salt to taste and Mix. Cook the water to a boil and then reduce its heat to low. Cook the chana dal on low heat until fully cooked and soft. This may take around 20-25 minutes. Once the chana dal is cooked, Turn off its heat and set it aside. In a suitable pan, heat the oil or ghee over medium heat. Add the chopped onion and green chilies and fry until the onions are translucent. Stir in the ginger paste and garlic paste and fry for another minute. Add the chopped tomato and fry for another minute. Add cumin powder, coriander powder, turmeric powder, and salt to taste. Mix and fry for another minute. Add the cooked chana dal to the pan and Mix. Cook the chana dal on medium heat for 5-7 minutes, with occasional stirring. Turn off its heat and garnish with coriander leaves. Serve the Bengali Style Chana Dal hot with steamed rice or chapati. Your Bangladeshi Style Chana Dal is now ready to be served! This dish is flavorful and nutritious and is a staple in Bangladeshi cuisine. Enjoy this delicious lentil dish with your family and friends.

# Bengali Bittergourd

**Preparation time:** 15 minutes
**Cook time:** 32 minutes
**Nutrition facts (per serving):** 161 Cal (0.4g fat, 0.2g protein, 1.1g fiber)

Bengali bitter gourd, also known as "uchche bhaja" in Bengali, is a popular vegetable dish in Bengali cuisine. It's typically prepared by slicing and frying bitter gourd in oil, then seasoning with spices such as turmeric, cumin, and coriander.

## Ingredients (2 servings)

2 medium-sized bitter gourds
1 onion, thinly sliced
1 teaspoon cumin seeds
1 teaspoon ginger paste
1 teaspoon garlic paste
1 teaspoon coriander powder
½ teaspoon cumin powder
½ teaspoon turmeric powder
½ teaspoon red chili powder
Salt, to taste
1 tablespoon mustard oil
Fresh coriander leaves, for garnishing

## Preparation

Wash the bitter gourds and slice them into thin rounds. Rub the bitter gourd rounds with salt and keep them aside for 10-15 minutes. This will help to remove the bitterness from the vegetable. After 15 minutes, rinse the bitter gourd rounds with cold water and pat them dry with a paper towel. In a suitable pan, heat the mustard oil over medium heat. Add the cumin seeds to the oil and fry until they start to splutter. Toss in the onions and sauté until they turn golden in color. Stir in the ginger paste and garlic paste to the pan and fry for a minute. Add the bitter gourd rounds to the pan and mix. Add the coriander powder, cumin powder, turmeric powder, red chili powder, and salt to taste. Mix.

Cover the pan and cook the bitter gourd on low heat for 20 minutes or until the vegetable is fully cooked. Once the bitter gourd is cooked, remove the lid and Continue cooking for 5-7 minutes to let any excess moisture evaporate. Turn off its heat and garnish with coriander leaves. Serve the Bengali-style bitter gourd hot with steamed rice or chapati. Your Bengali-style bitter gourd is now ready to be served! This dish is flavorful and nutritious, and the bitterness of the vegetable is balanced out by the spices and onions. Enjoy this delicious vegetable dish with your family and friends.

# Bengali Lamb Curry

**Preparation time:** 15 minutes
**Cook time:** 87 minutes
**Nutrition facts (per serving):** 221 Cal (11g fat, 4g protein, 1.4g fiber)

Bengali lamb curry, also known as Kosha Mangsho, is a slow-cooked mutton stew that's a popular dish in Bengali cuisine. It's made with tender pieces of mutton, spices, and aromatic ingredients like onions and ginger, and is usually served with steamed white rice or paratha.

**Ingredients (4 servings)**
2 lbs. lamb, cut into medium-sized pieces
2 onions, finely chopped
1 teaspoon ginger paste
1 teaspoon garlic paste
3 green chilies, slit lengthwise
1 teaspoon cumin powder
1 teaspoon coriander powder
½ teaspoon turmeric powder
½ teaspoon red chili powder
Salt, to taste
¼ cup mustard oil
2 bay leaves
3 cinnamon sticks
5 cardamom pods
3 cloves
2 cups water
Fresh coriander leaves, for garnishing

**Preparation**

In a suitable bowl, marinate the lamb with turmeric powder, cumin powder, coriander powder, red chili powder, ginger paste, garlic paste, and salt. Mix and keep aside for 30 minutes. Heat the mustard oil in a suitable pan over medium heat. Add the bay leaves, cinnamon sticks, cardamom pods, and cloves to the oil and fry for a minute. Stir in the chopped onions to the pan and fry until they turn golden in color. Add the marinated lamb to the pan and mix. Add the slit green chilies to the pan and Mix. Cover the pan and let the lamb cook on low heat for 30-40 minutes, with occasional stirring. Add 2 cups of water to the pan and mix. Cover the pan and cook the lamb for another 30-40 minutes or until fully cooked and the gravy thickens. Once the lamb is cooked, remove the lid and Continue cooking for 5-7 minutes to let any excess moisture evaporate. Turn off its heat and garnish with coriander leaves. Serve the Bengali-style lamb curry hot with steamed rice or chapati.

# Egg Masala Curry

**Preparation time:** 15 minutes
**Cook time:** 45 minutes
**Nutrition facts (per serving):** 317 Cal (17g fat, 5g protein, 0.8g fiber)

Egg masala curry is a flavorful Bangladeshi dish made with boiled eggs cooked in a spicy onion and tomato-based sauce. It's usually enjoyed with rice or bread and makes for a delicious and filling meal.

## Ingredients (3 servings)
6 boiled eggs, peeled and halved
2 onions, finely chopped
2 tomatoes, finely chopped
1 teaspoon ginger paste
1 teaspoon garlic paste
2 green chilies, slit lengthwise
½ teaspoon cumin powder
½ teaspoon coriander powder
½ teaspoon turmeric powder
½ teaspoon red chili powder
Salt, to taste
2 tablespoons vegetable oil
1 bay leaf
3 cloves
3 cardamom pods
1-inch cinnamon stick
1 cup water
Fresh coriander leaves, for garnishing

**Preparation**

Heat the vegetable oil in a suitable pan over medium heat. Add the bay leaf, cloves, cardamom pods, and cinnamon stick to the oil and fry for a minute. Stir in the chopped onions to the pan and fry until they turn golden in color. Stir in the ginger paste and garlic paste to the pan and sauté for a minute. Add the chopped tomatoes to the pan and Mix. Add the coriander powder, cumin powder, turmeric powder, red chili powder, and salt to the pan and mix. Add the slit green chilies to the pan and mix. Cover the pan and let the tomato mixture cook on low heat for 10-15 minutes, with occasional stirring. Add 1 cup of water to the pan and mix. Add the boiled egg halves to the pan and mix gently. Cover the pan and cook the egg masala curry for another 10-15 minutes, with occasional stirring. Once the curry is cooked, remove the lid and Continue cooking for 5-7 minutes to let any excess moisture evaporate. Turn off its heat and garnish with coriander leaves. Serve the egg masala curry hot with steamed rice or bread. Your egg masala curry is now ready to be served! This dish is creamy, flavorful, and perfect for a comforting meal. Enjoy!

# Prawn And Yellow Split Pea Curry

**Preparation time:** 15 minutes
**Cook time:** 40 minutes
**Nutrition facts (per serving):** 265 Cal (5g fat, 7g protein, 5g fiber)

This Yellow Split Pea Curry is a flavorful and protein-rich dish made with yellow split peas and fresh prawns. The dish is typically prepared with a blend of aromatic spices, onions, tomatoes, and coconut milk to create a rich and satisfying curry.

**Ingredients (4 servings)**
1 cup yellow split peas, soaked for 1 hour
1 lb. prawns, cleaned and deveined
1 onion, finely chopped
1 tomato, finely chopped
1 teaspoon ginger paste
1 teaspoon garlic paste
2 green chilies, slit lengthwise
1 teaspoon cumin powder
1 teaspoon coriander powder
½ teaspoon turmeric powder
½ teaspoon red chili powder
Salt, to taste
2 tablespoons vegetable oil
1 bay leaf
3 cloves
3 cardamom pods
1-inch cinnamon stick
1 cup water
Fresh coriander leaves, for garnishing

**Preparation**

Heat the vegetable oil in a suitable pan over medium heat. Add the bay leaf, cloves, cardamom pods, and cinnamon stick to the oil and fry for a minute. Toss in the chopped onions to the pan and fry until they turn golden in color. Stir in the ginger paste and garlic paste to the pan and fry for a minute. Add the chopped tomatoes to the pan and mix. Add the salt, cumin powder, red chili powder, coriander powder, turmeric powder to the pan and mix. Drain the soaked yellow split peas and add them to the pan. Mix. Add 1 cup of water to the pan and mix. Cover the pan and let the curry cook on low heat for 20 minutes, with occasional stirring. Add the cleaned and deveined prawns to the pan and mix gently. Cover this pan and cook the curry for another 5-7 minutes, until the prawns are cooked through. Once the curry is cooked, remove the lid and Continue cooking for 5-7 minutes to let any excess moisture evaporate. Turn off its heat and garnish with coriander leaves. Serve the Prawn and Yellow Split Pea Curry hot with steamed rice or bread. Enjoy this flavorful and comforting dish with family and friends!

# Tomato Bhurta

**Preparation time:** 15 minutes
**Cook time:** 30 minutes
**Nutrition facts (per serving):** 367 Cal (21g fat, 9g protein, 1.2g fiber)

Tomato Bhurta is a flavorful Bengali side dish made by roasting tomatoes and then mixing with spices and herbs. It can be enjoyed with rice or roti.

**Ingredients (2 servings)**
4 ripe tomatoes
1 onion, finely chopped
1 green chili, finely chopped
1 teaspoon ginger paste
1 teaspoon garlic paste
½ teaspoon turmeric powder
½ teaspoon cumin powder
½ teaspoon coriander powder
Salt, to taste
2 tablespoons vegetable oil
Fresh coriander leaves, for garnishing

**Preparation**
Cut the tomatoes into small pieces and mash them using any fork or a potato masher. Heat the vegetable oil in a suitable pan over medium heat. Stir in the chopped onions to the pan and fry until they turn golden in color. Stir in the ginger paste and garlic paste to the pan and fry for a minute. Add the chopped green chili to the pan and fry for a minute. Stir in the mashed tomatoes to the pan and mix. Add the turmeric powder,

cumin powder, coriander powder, and salt to the pan and mix. Cover the pan and let the Tomato Bhurta cook on low heat for 10-15 minutes, with occasional stirring. Once the Tomato Bhurta is cooked, remove the lid and Continue cooking for 5-7 minutes to let any excess moisture evaporate. Turn off its heat and garnish with coriander leaves. Serve the Tomato Bhurta hot with steamed rice or bread. Enjoy this simple and flavorful Bengali dish with family and friends!

# Bengali Chicken and Potato Curry

**Preparation time:** 15 minutes

**Cook time:** 40 minutes

**Nutrition facts (per serving):** 211 Cal (1.2g fat, 8g protein, 7g fiber)

Bengali Chicken and Potato Curry is a popular dish made with chicken and potatoes in a flavorful tomato-based sauce. It's usually served with steamed rice or Indian bread.

## Ingredients (2 servings)

1 lb. bone-in chicken pieces

3 medium-sized potatoes, peeled and cubed

1 onion, chopped

2 cloves garlic, minced

1-inch piece of ginger, minced

1 tomato, chopped

1 teaspoon cumin powder

1 teaspoon coriander powder

½ teaspoon turmeric powder

½ teaspoon chili powder

Salt, to taste

2 tablespoons vegetable oil

Water, as needed

Fresh coriander leaves, for garnishing

## Preparation

Heat the vegetable oil in a suitable pan over medium heat. Add the chopped onion to the pan and fry until it turns golden in color. Stir in the minced garlic and ginger to the pan and fry for a minute. Add the chopped tomato to the pan and fry for 2-3 minutes. Stir in the salt, cumin powder, coriander powder, turmeric powder, chili powder to the pan and mix. Place the chicken pieces in this pan and fry for 5-7 minutes or until the chicken turns brown. Stir in the cubed potatoes to the pan and mix. Add water to the pan until the chicken and potatoes are covered. Cover this pan and let it cook on low heat for 20-25 minutes, or until the chicken and potatoes are cooked through. Remove its lid and let the curry simmer for another 5-7 minutes until the gravy thickens. Turn off its heat and garnish with coriander leaves. Serve the Bengali Chicken and Potato Curry hot with steamed rice or bread. Enjoy this delicious and hearty Bengali dish with family and friends!

# Mutton Rezala

**Preparation time:** 15 minutes
**Cook time:** 2 hours 15 minutes
**Nutrition facts (per serving):** 211 Cal (1.2g fat, 8g protein, 7g fiber)

Mutton Rezala is a popular Bengali dish that originated in the Mughal era. It's a rich and flavorful curry made with tender pieces of mutton cooked in a fragrant white gravy.

## Ingredients (4 servings)

2 lbs. mutton, cut into small pieces

2 cups yogurt

1 cup onion paste

½ cup cashew paste

¼ cup poppy seed paste

2 tablespoons ginger paste

2 tablespoons garlic paste

2 tablespoons ghee or clarified butter

3 bay leaves

3 cardamom pods

3 cloves

1 cinnamon stick

1 teaspoon sugar

Salt, to taste

Fresh coriander leaves, for garnishing

**Preparation**

In a suitable bowl, mix together the yogurt, onion paste, cashew paste, poppy seed paste, ginger paste, and garlic paste until well combined. Heat the ghee in a suitable pot over medium heat. Add the bay leaves, cardamom pods, cloves, and cinnamon stick to the pot and fry for a few seconds until fragrant. Add the mutton pieces to the pot and fry for 10-15 minutes or until they turn brown. Add the yogurt mixture to the pot and mix. Add the sugar and salt to the pot and mix. Cover this pot and let it cook on low heat for 1-2 hours or until the mutton is tender and the gravy thickens. Once the mutton is cooked, Turn off its heat and leave for a few minutes. Garnish this Rezala with coriander leaves and serve hot with steamed rice or bread. Enjoy this delicious and aromatic Bengali Mutton Rezala with your loved ones!

# Prawn Malai Curry

**Preparation time:** 15 minutes
**Cook time:** 25 minutes
**Nutrition facts (per serving):** 382 Cal (13g fat, 9g protein, 6g fiber)

Prawn Malai Curry is a popular Bengali dish that blends the sweetness of coconut milk with the spiciness of Indian spices.

## Ingredients (4 servings)
1 lb. prawns, deveined and cleaned
1 cup coconut milk
1 onion, finely chopped
2 garlic cloves, minced
1-inch ginger, grated
2 green chilies, chopped
2 tablespoons mustard oil
1 teaspoon turmeric powder
1 teaspoon red chili powder
1 teaspoon cumin powder
1 teaspoon coriander powder
1 bay leaf
Salt, to taste
Fresh coriander leaves, for garnishing

## Preparation
Heat the mustard oil in a suitable pan over medium heat. Add the bay leaf, chopped onion, minced garlic, grated ginger, and chopped green chilies. Sauté for a few minutes until the onions are soft and translucent.

Add the turmeric powder, red chili powder, cumin powder, coriander powder, and salt. Mix and cook for a few more minutes. Add the prawns to the pan and Mix with the spices. Cook for 2-3 minutes. Add the coconut milk to the pan and stir well. Cook to a simmer and cook for 10-15 minutes until the curry thickens and the prawns are fully cooked. Once the prawns are cooked, Turn off its heat and leave for a few minutes. Garnish with coriander leaves and serve warm. Enjoy this delicious and creamy Prawn Malai Curry with your loved ones!

# Turmeric Fish Curry

**Preparation time:** 15 minutes
**Cook time:** 25 minutes
**Nutrition facts (per serving):** 259 Cal (5 g fat, 23g protein, 6g fiber)

Turmeric Fish Curry is a popular Bengali dish that's cooked with a blend of spices and bay leaf, giving it a distinct yellow color.

**Ingredients (2 servings)**
1 lb. fish, cut into pieces
1 onion, finely chopped
2 garlic cloves, minced
1-inch ginger, grated
2 green chilies, chopped
2 tablespoons mustard oil
1 teaspoon turmeric powder
1 teaspoon cumin powder
1 teaspoon coriander powder
1 bay leaf
Salt, to taste
Fresh coriander leaves, for garnishing

**Preparation**
Heat the mustard oil in a suitable pan over medium heat. Add the bay leaf, chopped onion, minced garlic, grated ginger, and chopped green chilies. Sauté for a few minutes until the onions are soft and translucent. Add the turmeric powder, cumin powder, coriander powder, and salt. Mix it and cook for a few more minutes. Keep the fish pieces in the pan

and mix with the spices. Cook for almost 2-3 minutes until the fish is slightly browned. Add 1 cup of water to this pan and cook to a boil. Cover this pan and cook for 10-15 minutes and the curry thickens. Once the fish is cooked, turn off its heat and leave for a few minutes. Garnish with coriander leaves and serve.

# Methi Machchi

**Preparation time:** 15 minutes
**Cook time:** 18 minutes
**Nutrition facts (per serving):** 382 Cal (13g fat, 9g protein, 6g fiber)

Methi Machchi is a delicious and healthy Bengali dish made with fish and fenugreek leaves.

### Ingredients (2 servings)
1 lb. fish, cut into pieces
1 bunch fenugreek leaves (methi), washed and chopped
2 onions, finely chopped
2 tomatoes, finely chopped
2 garlic cloves, minced
1-inch ginger, grated
2 green chilies, chopped
1 teaspoon cumin powder
1 teaspoon coriander powder
½ teaspoon turmeric powder
½ teaspoon red chili powder
Salt, to taste
3 tablespoons mustard oil
Water, as needed
Fresh coriander leaves, for garnishing

### Preparation
Heat the mustard oil in a suitable pan over medium heat. Add the chopped onion, minced garlic, grated ginger, and chopped green chilies.

Sauté for a few minutes until the onions are soft and translucent. Toss in the chopped tomatoes and cook until soft and mushy. Stir in cumin powder, coriander powder, turmeric powder, red chili powder, and salt. Mix well and cook for a few more minutes. Add the chopped fenugreek leaves and cook for 2-3 minutes until they wilt. Place the fish pieces in this pan and mix with the spices. Stir in water as needed to make a thick gravy. Cover this pan and cook for almost 15 minutes until the fish is completely cooked and the curry thickens. Once the fish is cooked, turn off its heat and leave for a few minutes. Garnish with coriander leaves and serve.

# Desserts

# Rasgulla

**Preparation time:** 15 minutes
**Cook time:** 19 minutes
**Nutrition facts (per serving):** 268 Cal (26g fat, 9g protein, 0.3g fiber)

Rasgulla is a popular Indian dessert made from chenna (cottage cheese) and soaked in a sugar syrup. It's round, spongy, and has a slightly chewy texture.

**Ingredients (4 servings)**
*Rasgulla Balls*
4 cups cow's milk
2 tablespoons lemon juice or vinegar
½ cup water
½ teaspoon cardamom powder
1 cup sugar

*Sugar Syrup*
2 cups water
1 ½ cups sugar
½ teaspoon cardamom powder

**Preparation**
Warm up the milk in a heavy-bottomed pan over medium heat and cook it to a gentle boil. Once the milk starts boiling, add lemon juice or vinegar and stir well until the milk curdles and the whey (transparent liquid) separates. Turn off its heat and leave it to sit for a minute. Then strain the curdled milk using a muslin cloth or a fine mesh strainer to separate the

paneer (cheese) from the whey. Rinse the paneer under running water to remove any traces of lemon juice or vinegar.

Squeeze out the excess water gently from the paneer. Place the paneer on a flat surface, such as a clean kitchen counter, and knead it with your hand for about 5 minutes until smooth and soft. This helps in removing any remaining moisture and makes the paneer pliable. Divide the paneer into small lemon-sized balls and roll them between your palms to make smooth balls without any cracks. In a separate pan, prepare the sugar syrup by adding water, sugar, and cardamom powder.

Cook it to a boil on a simmer for 5-7 minutes until the sugar dissolves completely and the syrup becomes slightly thick. Gently slide the paneer balls into the simmering sugar syrup and cover the pan with a lid. Let them cook on medium heat for almost 10-12 minutes until the balls double in size and become spongy. Turn off its heat and let the Rasgulla balls cool down in the sugar syrup for a while. Once cooled, carefully remove the Rasgulla balls from the sugar syrup and keep them in a serving bowl. Chill the Rasgulla in the refrigerator for a few hours before serving. Serve chilled and enjoy the soft, spongy, and sweet Rasgulla as a delicious Bengali dessert!

# Sweetened Paneer

**Preparation time:** 15 minutes
**Cook time:** 12 minutes
**Nutrition facts (per serving):** 249 Cal (7g fat, 2g protein, 3g fiber)

Sandesh is a popular Bengali sweet made from sweetened paneer (cottage cheese) and various flavorings such as cardamom, saffron, and pistachios.

## Ingredients (4 servings)
4 cups cow's milk
2 tablespoons lemon juice or vinegar
½ cup powdered sugar
¼ teaspoon cardamom powder
A few strands of saffron (optional)
Chopped nuts (almonds, pistachios, or cashews), for garnish

## Preparation
Heat the milk in a heavy-bottomed pan over medium heat and cook it to a gentle boil. Once the milk starts boiling, add lemon juice or vinegar and stir well until the milk curdles and the whey (transparent liquid) separates. Turn off its heat and leave it to sit for a minute. Then strain the curdled milk using a muslin cloth or a fine mesh strainer to separate the paneer (cheese) from the whey.

Rinse the paneer under running water to remove any traces of lemon juice or vinegar. Squeeze out the excess water gently from the paneer. Place the paneer in a suitable pan and cook it on low heat for 3-4 minutes, stirring constantly, until it becomes slightly dry and crumbly. Add powdered sugar, cardamom powder, and saffron (if using) to the paneer and mix. Cook the paneer mixture on low heat for another 2-3 minutes, stirring continuously, until it thickens and leaves the sides of the pan. Turn off its heat and let the paneer mixture cool down to room temperature. Once the paneer mixture is cool enough to handle, divide it into small portions and shape them into small discs, balls, or any desired shape.

Garnish the Sandesh with chopped nuts on top. Chill the Sandesh in the refrigerator for at least 1 hour before serving to allow it to set. Serve the chilled Sandesh as a delightful Bengali dessert and enjoy its creamy, sweet, and rich flavor!

# Mishti Doi

**Preparation time:** 15 minutes
**Cook time:** 50 minutes
**Nutrition facts (per serving):** 211 Cal (1.2g fat, 8g protein, 7g fiber)

Mishti Doi, or sweetened yogurt, is a popular Bengali dessert known for its creamy, rich, and sweet flavor.

## Ingredients (4 servings)
4 cups full-fat milk
½ cup condensed milk
½ cup sugar, powdered
½ teaspoon cardamom powder
A pinch of saffron strands (optional)
Chopped nuts (such as almonds, pistachios, or cashews), for garnish

## Preparation
Heat the milk in a heavy-bottomed pan over medium heat and cook it to a boil. Reduce its heat to low and let the milk simmer for about 30 minutes, with occasional stirring, until it thickens and reduces to about half of its original volume. Add the condensed milk and powdered sugar to the milk, and mix until the sugar dissolves completely. Continue to simmer the milk mixture on low heat for another 10-15 minutes, with occasional stirring, until it thickens to a creamy consistency. Add the cardamom powder and saffron strands (if using), and Mix.

Turn off its heat and let the sweetened milk mixture cool down to room temperature. Once the milk mixture is cool enough, pour it into clean and dry earthenware pots or glass containers. Cover the pots or containers with a clean cloth and let them sit undisturbed in a warm place for 6-8 hours, or until the yogurt sets and thickens to your desired consistency. Once the Mishti Doi is set, refrigerate it for at least 1-2 hours to chill and firm up. Garnish the chilled Mishti Doi with chopped nuts on top before serving. Serve the chilled Mishti Doi as a delightful Bengali dessert and enjoy its creamy, sweet, and aromatic taste!

# Payesh

**Preparation time:** 15 minutes
**Cook time:** 25 minutes
**Nutrition facts (per serving):** 367 Cal (21g fat, 9g protein, 1.2g fiber)

Payesh, also known as Bengali Rice Pudding, is a classic Bengali dessert made with rice, milk, sugar, and flavored with cardamom and nuts. It's often served during special occasions and memorable festivals.

## Ingredients (4 servings)

½ cup Basmati rice, rinsed
4 cups full-fat milk
½ cup sugar or adjust to taste
½ teaspoon cardamom powder
A pinch of saffron strands (optional)
Nuts (almonds, cashews, pistachios), chopped, for garnish

## Preparation

In a heavy-bottomed pan, add the soaked and drained rice along with 2 cups of water. Cook it to a boil over medium heat. Reduce its heat to low and let the rice cook until it's soft and fully cooked. Drain any excess water and set the cooked rice aside. In the same pan, add the milk and cook it to a boil over medium heat. Reduce its heat to low and let the milk simmer, stirring frequently, until it thickens and reduces to about half of its original volume.

Add the cooked rice to the thickened milk and stir well. Stir in sugar and cardamom powder to the pan and mix. Continue cooking for 10-15 minutes on low heat, stirring frequently, until the Payesh thickens to a creamy consistency. Add saffron strands (if using) and mix. Turn off its heat and let the Payesh cool down to room temperature. Once the Payesh is cool enough, refrigerate it for at least 1-2 hours to chill and firm up. Garnish the chilled Payesh with chopped nuts on top before serving. Serve the chilled Payesh as a delicious Bengali dessert and enjoy its creamy, aromatic, and sweet taste!

# Chomchom

**Preparation time:** 15 minutes

**Cook time:** 43 minutes

**Nutrition facts (per serving):** 265 Cal (5g fat, 7g protein, 5g fiber)

Chomchom is a popular Bengali dessert made with fresh paneer (cottage cheese) that's shaped into oval balls, cooked in sugar syrup, and then soaked in a sweet syrup flavored with cardamom and saffron. It is a delicious and indulgent sweet treat that's often served during special festivals and distinct occasions.

## Ingredients (6 servings)

### Chomchom Balls

4 cups milk

2 tablespoons lemon juice or vinegar

1 cup sugar

2 cups water

A few strands of saffron

½ teaspoon cardamom powder

Chopped nuts (almonds, pistachios), for garnish

### Sugar Syrup

2 cups sugar

4 cups water

A few strands of saffron

½ teaspoon cardamom powder

**Preparation**

Heat the milk in a suitable pan over medium heat until it boils. Add lemon juice or vinegar to the boiling milk and stir gently until the milk curdles and the whey separates. Turn off its heat and leave for a few minutes. Line a strainer with any muslin cloth and strain the curdled milk to separate the paneer (cheese) from the whey. Rinse the paneer under running water to remove any lemony or acidic taste.

Gather the muslin cloth containing the paneer and squeeze out any excess water. Place the paneer on a clean surface and knead it your hand for about 5-7 minutes. Divide the paneer into small portions and shape them into small oval balls (Chomchom).In a suitable pot, add sugar and water for the sugar syrup and cook it to a boil over medium heat.Add saffron and cardamom powder to this sugar syrup and Cook it on a simmer for about 5 minutes.

Gently add the paneer balls to the simmering sugar syrup and let them cook for about 20 minutes, turning them occasionally for even cooking. Turn off its heat and let the paneer balls soak in the sugar syrup for another 2-3 hours, allowing them to absorb the flavors and sweetness of the syrup. Garnish the Chomchom with chopped nuts on top before serving. Serve the Chomchom chilled, along with some syrup, and enjoy the soft, spongy, and syrup-soaked cheese balls as a delightful Bengali dessert!

# Pantua

**Preparation time:** 15 minutes
**Cook time:** 15 minutes
**Nutrition facts (per serving):** 221 Cal (11g fat, 4g protein, 1.4g fiber)

Pantua is a popular Bengali dessert that is similar to Gulab Jamun, a popular Indian sweet. It's made with khoya (milk solids), semolina (Suji), and flour, which are deep-fried and then soaked in a nicely made sugar syrup flavored with cardamom and rose water. Pantua is known for its soft and melt-in-your-mouth texture, and it is often served during festivals and special occasions.

## Ingredients (6 servings)
### Pantua Balls
1 cup khoya (milk solids)
¼ cup semolina (Suji)
¼ cup all-purpose flour (maida)
A pinch of baking soda
1 tablespoon ghee (clarified butter)
Milk or water, as needed for kneading

### Sugar Syrup
2 cups sugar
2 cups water
½ teaspoon cardamom powder
½ teaspoon rose water

Vegetable oil or ghee, for deep frying

## Preparation

In a suitable mixing bowl, crumble the khoya (milk solids) with your fingers. Add semolina, all-purpose flour, baking soda, and ghee to the crumbled khoya. Mix all the recipe ingredients together to form a smooth dough. If needed, add a little milk or water to bring the prepared dough together. The prepared dough should be soft and pliable. Cover the prepared dough with some damp cloth and leave for 10-15 minutes.

Meanwhile, in a separate saucepan, prepare the sugar syrup by combining sugar, water, cardamom powder, and rose water. Cook it to a boil over medium heat, with occasional stirring until the sugar dissolves. Once the sugar syrup comes to a rolling boil, Reduce its heat to low and Cook it on a simmer for 5-7 minutes until it thickens slightly. Turn off its heat and set aside. Heat vegetable oil or ghee in a suitable deep frying pan over medium heat.

While the oil is heating, divide the prepared dough into equally-small portions and shape them into smooth balls. Once the oil or ghee is hot, carefully add the prepared dough balls to the hot oil and fry them on medium low to medium heat until golden in color and crispy on the outside. Remove the fried Pantua balls from the oil using any slotted spoon. Immediately transfer the hot Pantua balls to the prepared sugar syrup and leave them to soak for 2-3 hours, allowing them to absorb the flavors and sweetness of the syrup. Garnish the Pantua with chopped nuts (such as pistachios, almonds) on top before serving. Serve the Pantua warm or chilled, along with some syrup, and enjoy the soft and delicious Bengali dessert!

# Sondesh

**Preparation time:** 15 minutes

**Cook time:** 7 minutes

**Nutrition facts (per serving):** 317 Cal (17g fat, 5g protein, 0.8g fiber)

Sondesh is a popular Bengali dessert that is a variation of Sandesh. It is made with fresh paneer (cottage cheese) or chhena, and is often flavored with cardamom or saffron, and sweetened with sugar. Sondesh has a crumbly yet melt-in-your-mouth texture and is often shaped into small discs or balls before serving.

## Ingredients (6 servings)

2 cups fresh paneer (cottage cheese) or chhena

½ cup sugar, powdered

½ teaspoon cardamom powder

A few strands of saffron (optional)

Nuts (pistachios, almonds), chopped, for garnish

## Preparation

In a suitable mixing bowl, crumble the fresh paneer or chhena with your fingers. Add the powdered sugar, cardamom powder, and saffron strands (if using) to the crumbled paneer or chhena. Mix all the ingredients together until combined and the prepared mixture becomes smooth. Transfer the prepared mixture to a non-stick pan or a heavy-bottomed pan and cook on low heat, stirring continuously. Cook for 5-7 minutes until the prepared mixture thickens. Turn off its heat and let the mixture cool slightly. Once the prepared mixture is cool enough to handle, divide it into small portions and shape them into discs or balls. Garnish the

Sondesh with chopped nuts (such as pistachios, almonds) on top. Let the Sondesh cool completely and then refrigerate for at least 1-2 hours to set. Serve the Sondesh chilled and enjoy the delicious Bengali dessert!

# Nolen Gurer Payesh

**Preparation time:** 15 minutes
**Cook time:** 50 minutes
**Nutrition facts (per serving):** 202 Cal (7g fat, 6g protein, 1.3g fiber)

Nolen Gurer Payesh is a traditional Bengali dessert made with rice, milk, and Nolen Gur, which is date palm jaggery. It's a rich and creamy rice pudding that's often prepared during special festivals and festive occasions in Bengal.

## Ingredients (4 servings)
½ cup Basmati rice
4 cups whole milk
½ cup Nolen Gur (date palm jaggery), grated or chopped
½ teaspoon cardamom powder
A pinch of saffron strands (optional)
Chopped nuts (cashews, almonds, pistachios), for garnish

## Preparation
Wash the Basmati rice in water and drain. In a heavy-bottomed pan, add the washed rice and milk. Cook it to a boil on medium heat. Reduce its heat to low and let the rice and milk simmer, with occasional stirring. Cook the rice in milk until soft and fully cooked, and the milk thickens to a creamy consistency. This may take about 30-40 minutes. Add the grated or chopped Nolen Gur (date palm jaggery) to the pan and mix. Let it cook on a simmer for a few more minutes until the jaggery melts completely and gets incorporated into the rice and milk.

Add the cardamom powder and saffron strands (if using) to the pan and mix. Turn off its heat and let the Nolen Gurer Payesh cool to room temperature. Once the Payesh has cooled, transfer it to a serving bowl and garnish with nuts (such as cashews, almonds, pistachios) on top. You can serve Nolen Gurer Payesh chilled or at room temperature, as per your preference. Enjoy the rich and creamy Nolen Gurer Payesh, a beloved Bengali dessert, and savor the flavors of Nolen Gur!

# Langcha

**Preparation time:** 15 minutes
**Cook time:** 15 minutes
**Nutrition facts (per serving):** 393 Cal (18g g fat, 9g protein, 3g fiber)

Langcha is a popular Bengali dessert that consists of deep-fried and syrup-soaked sweet dough balls. It's similar to Gulab Jamun, but the shape and texture of Langcha are slightly different.

**Ingredients (6 servings)**
*Dough Balls*
1 cup khoya (milk solids)
½ cup all-purpose flour (maida)
¼ teaspoon baking soda
1 tablespoon ghee (clarified butter)
A pinch of cardamom powder

*Sugar Syrup*
1 cup sugar
1 cup water
A few drops of rose water (optional)
A few saffron strands (optional)

Oil, for deep frying

**Preparation**
In a suitable mixing bowl, crumble the khoya (milk solids) with your fingers or grate it. Add all-purpose flour, baking soda, ghee, and

cardamom powder to the bowl. Mix to form a smooth dough. Divide this prepared dough into small portions and shape them into small cylindrical or oval-shaped balls. In a suitable deep pan, heat oil for deep frying over medium heat. Carefully add the shaped dough balls to the hot oil and fry them until golden and crispy on the outside. Once the prepared dough balls are fried, remove them from the oil using any slotted spoon. In a separate saucepan, combine sugar and water to make the sugar syrup. Keep it on medium heat and let it come to a boil. Reduce its heat to low and simmer the sugar syrup for about 5-7 minutes until it thickens slightly. Add rose water and saffron strands (if using) to the sugar syrup and Mix. Drop the fried dough balls into the hot sugar syrup and leave them to soak for about 1-2 hours. The prepared dough balls will absorb the sugar syrup and become soft and syrupy. Garnish Langcha with some chopped nuts (such as pistachios, almonds) if desired. Serve Langcha as a sweet and delicious Bengali dessert. Enjoy the deep-fried and syrup-soaked sweet dough balls!

# Malpua

**Preparation time:** 15 minutes
**Cook time:** 15 minutes
**Nutrition facts (per serving):** 181 Cal (6g fat, 2.4g protein, 0.6g fiber)

Malpua is a popular Bengali dessert that consists of deep-fried pancakes made from a batter of all-purpose flour, milk, and sugar. These pancakes are super crispy on the outside and soft on the inside, and are usually soaked in a sugar syrup for added sweetness.

## Ingredients (6 servings)
### Pancake Batter
1 cup all-purpose flour (maida)
¼ cup semolina (sooji/rava)
¼ cup milk powder
¼ cup sugar
½ teaspoon cardamom powder
½ teaspoon fennel seeds (Saunf)
A pinch of baking soda
1 cup milk
Ghee or oil, for frying

### Sugar Syrup
1 cup sugar
1 cup water
A few saffron strands (optional)
½ teaspoon cardamom powder

Chopped nuts (almonds, pistachios), chopped, for garnish

## Preparation

In a suitable mixing bowl, combine the all-purpose flour, semolina, milk powder, sugar, cardamom powder, fennel seeds, and baking soda. Mix. Gradually add the milk to the bowl and whisk this batter until it becomes smooth and lump-free. The consistency of this batter should be similar to that of a suitable pancake batter. Heat the ghee or the oil in a shallow pan or a kadai (deep frying pan) over medium heat. Once the ghee or the oil is hot, drop spoonfuls of this batter into the pan to make small pancakes. You can make them in any shape, such as round or oval.

Fry the prepared pancakes on low to medium heat until golden. Flip them carefully using a spatula. Once the pancakes are fried, remove them from the pan. In a separate saucepan, combine sugar and water to make the sugar syrup. Keep it on medium heat and let it come to a boil. Reduce its heat to low and simmer the sugar syrup for about 5-7 minutes until it thickens slightly. Add saffron strands (if using) and cardamom powder to the sugar syrup and Mix well. Drop the fried pancakes (Malpua) into the hot sugar syrup and leave them to soak for a few minutes until they absorb the syrup and become soft. Garnish Malpua with some chopped nuts (if desired) and serve them warm as a delicious Bengali dessert.

# Pani Walalu

**Preparation time:** 20 minutes

**Cook time:** 25 minutes

**Nutrition facts (per serving):** 311 Cal (9g fat, 2g protein, 0g fiber)

If you're sweet lover, then this Pani Walalu recipe is the right fit for you. Try this at home and serve your cravings.

**Ingredients (12 servings)**

2 cups Urad Dal

1 cup rice flour

2 ½ cups coconut milk

Salt, to taste

4 glasses of superior Kithul treacle

1 cup water

**Preparation**

On a piece of clean muslin fabric, punch a circular hole with a diameter of ⅕ inch, and sew around the perimeter. Drain the water after soaking the urad dhal in it for the night. Utilizing a blender, make a thick paste out of it. Mix rice flour and the paste, and add 1 cup of thick coconut milk. When the batter is neither too thick nor too watery, add more flour or water. It should resemble perfectly mashed potatoes in texture. Add salt to your liking. A big frying pan with medium heat is used to heat the oil. Squeeze the batter into the oil in circular motions to create a coiled design, using the hole in the cloth as a nozzle. Until golden brown, fry. In the meantime, heat the treacle until little bubbles start to appear in the liquid. Treacle shouldn't be heated too much. After draining the oil, dip the coils in boiling treacle and let them soak for a while. Remove the Pani Walalu coils and keep them for up to a week in a saucepan with treacle.

# Athirasa

**Preparation time:** 10 minutes

**Cook time:** 18 minutes

**Nutrition facts (per serving):** 284 Cal (8g fat, 2g protein, 1g fiber)

In Bangladesh, Athirasa is a highly popular Awurudu sweet. Athirasa was made for the Tamil and Sinhala New Years in almost all homes.

**Ingredients (12 servings)**

1 lb. rice flour

10 ½ oz. sugar

¼ oz. of fennel seeds

2 teaspoons salt

Kappi (cracked rice), as needed

Whole-wheat flour, as needed

Coconut nectar (optional)

Oil, for deep-frying

**Preparation**

Add the cracked rice to a frying pan and cook over medium heat until it turns light brown. To thoroughly crush fennel seeds, fry them for about 1 minute. After that, add a tiny amount of sugar to a suitable skillet and stir continually while allowing it to melt over medium heat. Add 1 cup of hot water once the sugar has thoroughly melted and turned a deep brown color. Next, add the remaining sugar and blend well.

Mix thoroughly after adding salt. Cook this sugar syrup over medium heat until it reaches the proper consistency. Pour a tiny bit of this sugar syrup onto a spoon and consume it. If the sugar mixture is dripping in a thick lime to the level. Fill 1 cup with a half-cup of sugar syrup and set it aside. Use this when including flour. Mix thoroughly after adding coconut honey. After about 1 minute, extinguish the flame. Fennel seeds and cracked rice should also be added. Mix in rice flour a bit at a time. Don't add all of the rice flour at once. It will be challenging to correctly mix this if you do this. Mix in the all-purpose flour. Touch the mixture with your fingertips after adding all the flour. The mixture is at the proper amount if it doesn't stick to your fingertips.

Transfer the flour mixture into the board after coating it with oil. Then add a small amount of water to your pan along with this combination. Incorporate this viscous liquid completely into your flour mixture and stir until it's nice and smooth. Start by rubbing a little coconut oil onto your palms before beginning to make kawum. Make little balls first, then set them aside. After that, press these balls to create biscuit-like forms. 1 by one, drop the prepared kawum into the hot oil. Wait until the next kawum comes up after placing the first one. Your kawum will stab each other if you don't.

Remove the kawum from the oil once it turns a golden brown color and keep it on a net or piece of paper. The rest of your mixture should be treated similarly. Put a dish or a tiny cup at the bottom of the container you're using to hold your prepared kawum, then arrange the kawum around it. Because Athirasa has more oil than other kawum, we do this. The kawum at the bottom of the container will absorb more oil if you simply store them there.

# Drinks

# Aam Panna

**Preparation time:** 15 minutes
**Nutrition facts (per serving):** 161 Cal (0.4g fat, 0.2g protein, 1.1g fiber)

Here's a good refreshing summer drink made with raw mangoes, sugar, and spices. It's a popular drink in Bangladesh and is known for its sweet, tangy, and slightly spicy flavor.

## Ingredients (1 serving)

1 large raw mango, peeled and chopped
½ cup sugar
½ teaspoon black salt
½ teaspoon roasted cumin powder
A pinch of black pepper powder
Mint leaves, for garnish
Ice cubes, to taste

## Preparation

Boil the chopped raw mangoes in water until soft and cooked. Drain the water and let the mangoes cool down. Once cooled, blend the mangoes in a suitable blender with the sugar, black salt, roasted cumin powder, and black pepper powder to a smooth puree. Add the water to adjust the consistency and taste. Serve Aam Panna chilled with ice cubes, garnished with mint leaves.

# Gondhoraj Lebu Soda

**Preparation time:** 15 minutes
**Nutrition facts (per serving):** 130 Cal (3g fat, 2 protein, 0.3g fiber)

Gondhoraj Lebu Soda is a refreshing and tangy lemon-lime soda from West Bengal, India, made with the juice of the aromatic Gondhoraj Lebu or "king of limes," mixed with soda water and sugar syrup, and served over ice.

## Ingredients (1 serving)

Juice of 1 Gondhoraj Lebu (Bengali fragrant lime)

¼ cup sugar

Soda water, to taste

Ice cubes, to taste

## Preparation

In a glass, add the Gondhoraj Lebu juice and sugar. Stir well until the sugar dissolves. Add the soda water to your serving glass and stir gently. Add the ice cubes and serve Gondhoraj Lebu Soda chilled.

# Borhani

**Preparation time:** 15 minutes
**Nutrition facts (per serving):** 145 Cal (4.4g fat, 0.3g protein, 0g fiber)

Borhani is a popular traditional drink in Bangladesh made with yogurt, mint, coriander, chili, and other spices. It's usually served as a refreshing drink during special occasions and holiday celebrations.

## Ingredients (1 serving)

1 cup plain yogurt
½ teaspoon roasted cumin powder
½ teaspoon black salt
¼ teaspoon black pepper powder
A pinch of salt
A pinch of sugar
Fresh coriander leaves, for garnish
Ice cubes, to taste

## Preparation

In a suitable bowl, whisk together the plain yogurt, roasted cumin powder, black salt, black pepper powder, salt, and sugar until well combined. Add the water to adjust the consistency and taste. Serve Borhani chilled with ice cubes, garnished with coriander leaves.

# Shorbot

**Preparation time:** 15 minutes

**Nutrition facts (per serving):** 172 Cal (6g fat, 0.3g protein, 0g fiber)

Shorbot is a popular sweet drink in Bangladesh made with fruits, spices, sugar, and water. It's served chilled and is a refreshing drink in hot weather.

## Ingredients (1 serving)

2 tablespoons rose syrup

Juice of 1 lemon

¼ cup sugar

Water, to taste

Ice cubes, to taste

## Preparation

In a pitcher, mix together the rose syrup, lemon juice, sugar, and water. Stir well until the sugar dissolves. Add the ice cubes and serve Shorbot chilled.

# Lassi

**Preparation time:** 15 minutes
**Nutrition facts (per serving):** 182 Cal (0.4g fat, 0.7g protein, 1.4g fiber)

Lassi is a traditional yogurt-based drink from the Indian subcontinent. It's a good refreshing drink that can be quite sweet or savory, and can be flavored with fruit, spices, or herbs.

## Ingredients (1 serving)

1 cup plain yogurt
¼ cup sugar
½ teaspoon cardamom powder
½ teaspoon roasted cumin powder
Water, to taste
Ice cubes, to taste

## Preparation

In a suitable blender, combine the plain yogurt, sugar or salt, and optional flavorings such as cardamom powder or roasted cumin powder. Add the water to adjust the consistency and taste. Blend until smooth and frothy. Serve chilled with ice cubes.

If you liked Bangladeshi recipes, discover to how cook DELICIOUS recipes from **Balkan** countries!

Within these pages, you'll learn 35 authentic recipes from a Balkan cook. These aren't ordinary recipes you'd find on the Internet, but recipes that were closely guarded by our Balkan mothers and passed down from generation to generation.

Main Dishes, Appetizers, and Desserts included!

If you want to learn how to make Croatian green peas stew, and 32 other authentic Balkan recipes, then start with our book!

Order at www.balkanfood.org/cook-books/ for only $2,99!

Maybe Hungarian cuisine?

If you're a **Mediterranean** dieter who wants to know the secrets of the Mediterranean diet, dieting, and cooking, then you're about to discover how to master cooking meals on a Mediterranean diet right now!

In fact, if you want to know how to make Mediterranean food, then this new e-book - "The 30-minute Mediterranean diet" - gives you the answers to many important questions and challenges every Mediterranean dieter faces, including:

- How can I succeed with a Mediterranean diet?
- What kind of recipes can I make?
- What are the key principles to this type of diet?
- What are the suggested weekly menus for this diet?
- Are there any cheat items I can make?

... and more!

If you're serious about cooking meals on a Mediterranean diet and you really want to know how to make Mediterranean food, then you need to grab a copy of "The 30-minute Mediterranean diet" right now.

Prepare **111 recipes with several ingredients in less than 30 minutes**!

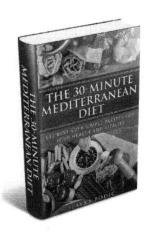

Order at www.balkanfood.org/cook-books/ for only $2,99!

What could be better than a home-cooked meal? Maybe only a **Greek** homemade meal.

Do not get discouraged if you have no Greek roots or friends. Now you can make a Greek food feast in your kitchen.

This ultimate Greek cookbook offers you 111 best dishes of this cuisine! From more famous gyros to more exotic *Kota Kapama* this cookbook keeps it easy and affordable.

All the ingredients necessary are wholesome and widely accessible. The author's picks are as flavorful as they are healthy. The dishes described in this cookbook are "what Greek mothers have made for decades."

Full of well-balanced and nutritious meals, this handy cookbook includes many vegan options. Discover a plethora of benefits of Mediterranean cuisine, and you may fall in love with cooking at home.

Inspired by a real food lover, this collection of delicious recipes will taste buds utterly satisfied.

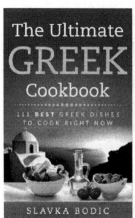

Order at www.balkanfood.org/cook-books/ for only $2,99!

Maybe some Swedish meatballs ?

Maybe to try exotic **Syrian** cuisine?

From succulent *sarma*, soups, warm and cold salads to delectable desserts, the plethora of flavors will satisfy the most jaded foodie. Have a taste of a new culture with this **traditional Syrian cookbook**.

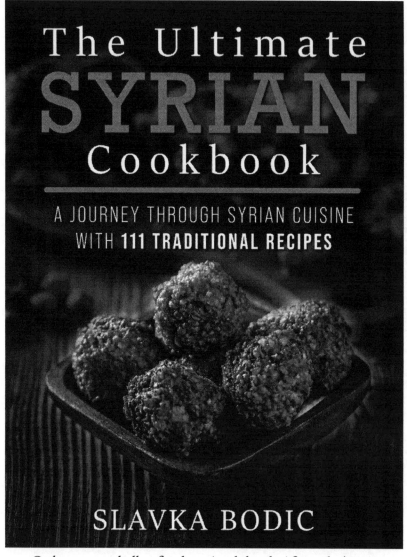

Maybe **Polish** cuisine?

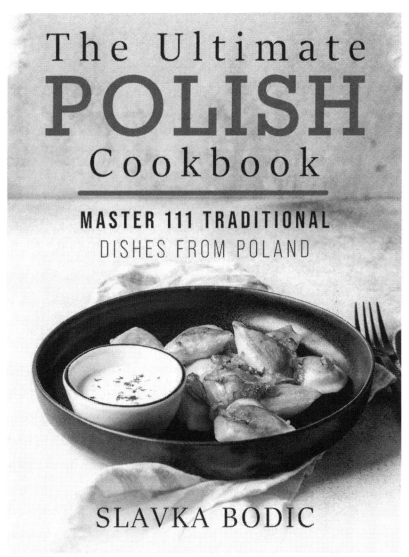

Or **Peruvian?**

# ONE LAST THING

If you enjoyed this book or found it useful, I'd be very grateful if you could find the time to post a short review on Amazon. Your support really does make a difference and I read all the reviews personally, so I can get your feedback and make this book even better.

Thanks again for your support!

Please send me your feedback at

www.balkanfood.org